The STRONG Family

Insight for Living
Insights and Application Workbook

From the Bible-Teaching Ministry of

Charles R. Swindoll

INSIGHT FOR LIVING

The Strong Family Workbook

Charles R. Swindoll has devoted his life to the clear, practical teaching and application of God's Word and His grace. A pastor at heart, Chuck has served as senior pastor to congregations in Texas, Massachusetts, and California. He currently pastors Stonebriar Community Church in Frisco, Texas, but Chuck's listening audience extends far beyond a local church body. As a leading program in Christian broadcasting, *Insight for Living* airs in major Christian radio markets around the world, reaching churched and unchurched people groups in languages they can understand. Chuck's extensive writing ministry has also served the body of Christ worldwide, and his leadership as president and now chancellor of Dallas Theological Seminary has helped prepare and equip a new generation for ministry. Chuck and Cynthia, his partner in life and ministry, have four grown children and ten grandchildren.

Based on the original outlines, charts, and transcripts of Charles R. Swindoll's sermons, the original study guide text was written by Ken Gire, revised by Lee Hough, and expanded into this workbook by Marla Alupoaicei, Mark Gaither, and Suzanne Keffer, all Th.M. graduates of Dallas Theological Seminary. Contextual support material was provided by the Creative Ministries Department of Insight for Living.

Editor in Chief: Cynthia Swindoll   **Editors:** Greg Smith, Amy Snedaker
Director: Mark Gaither   **Copy Editors:** Maridee Dietzel, Cari Harris, Mike Penn

Contents

Section Three: Weathering the Storm

A Letter from Chuck

Dear Friends:

Quite some time ago *The Strong Family* series was first aired on *Insight for Living.* A lot of water has flowed beneath the bridge since then. So much has changed in our culture, our world . . . our own family! The four Swindoll children now face the challenges and joys of raising their own families. From my perspective as a grandfather, I can say without hesitation that the changes in our culture over the last two decades haven't made their job any easier.

While the perils have changed, thankfully, the truths of Scripture have not. And, as long as there are people, there will be the need for practical teaching on the family sourced in the Scriptures. I am convinced more than ever that God created the family as a means of bringing people to Himself and holding them close.

Nearly every narrative in the Bible turns on family dynamics that contribute either to the success or failure of the central character. As you will recall, the Bible often says of a ruler, "He walked in all the ways of his father." That repeated epitaph for kings, good and bad, drives the point home: *Parents usually produce children after their own image.*

How sobering is *that*? Let's face it; the task is too big for us to do alone. Fortunately, God doesn't expect us to. He's provided everything we need to know in the pages of the Bible, and He promised His Holy Spirit to guide us . . . if only we will pay attention.

This workbook will help you learn and apply God's timeless truths as you steer your family through whatever rocks or reefs you may be navigating these days. But don't merely read the chapters. Determine now to roll up your sleeves and do the work. Carefully consider each question. Put the projects in motion. Pay attention to what you can learn about yourself and each member of your family. Remain sensitive to the Spirit's prompting. He wants to do a great work in you and through you . . . just wait and see.

My hope is that you will allow your heavenly Father to transform your family from where you are today into a strong family in the days ahead. Exciting thought, isn't it?

Chuck Swindoll

Charles R. Swindoll

How to Use *The Strong Family* Workbook

We are confident that this workbook from our Insights and Application line of biblical resources will help you transform your family into a strong family—one that won't wash away with each wave of change. Use this workbook as a tool in your personal devotions, small-group studies, or church curriculum.

Personal Devotions—While we encourage couples, and even families, to study together, we often find that one person obeying Scripture can have remarkable impact on the entire household. This workbook will help you become the anchor your family needs.

Small-Group Bible Studies—Join forces with other couples or groups. You'll encourage and learn from each other as you complete the exercises and apply the truths you discover.

Church Curriculum—Use this workbook to provide training to families struggling to raise children in a culture that is hostile to Christian principles. Let the questions and exercises transform your classroom into a workshop with practical, relevant tools for building strong families.

Look for these special features in *The Strong Family* Workbook:

Getting to the Root lets you tap into the original meanings of Hebrew and Greek words from the text.

In Other Words provides thought-provoking, applicable quotes from various authors to help you consider biblical principles from different perspectives.

Family Huddle provides practical exercises that will help you apply Scriptural principles specifically and strategically. The purpose of a huddle in football is to gather the team for a quick time-out—to assess the current situation and plan what to do next. It keeps each player focused on working together to accomplish what everyone wants: *victory*. The Family Huddle exercises can be done alone, with your spouse, or in some cases, with your entire family. They are designed to help you assess your family's needs so you can celebrate each member's successes and discover struggles before they become crises.

The STRONG Family

INTRODUCTION

Things Have Changed

In 1980, futurist author Alvin Toffler reported that the "traditional" family, consisting of a working father and home-keeping mother raising two of their own children, had long been an "ideal" of the past. By the time of that writing, only seven percent of all households fit that model,[1] and today, the Census Bureau doesn't even have a category for it. In the nineties, the number of blended families—households with children from previous marriages—overtook those where mom and dad reared their own children together. And in 2000, one out of every four households with children had a single mom or dad at the helm. Now, people are waiting until much later in life to marry.

As a result of these and other trends, married couples with children have become the slowest growing category of families over the last thirty years, with single-parent families becoming the fastest in the last ten. This only confirms that the first sermon in *The Strong Family* series, titled "An Endangered Species?" is as timely now as ever.

Sure, things have changed, but we were warned. Look at what Toffler had to say in his book *The Third Wave* more than twenty-five years ago.

> Most people . . . assume the world they know will last indefinitely. They find it difficult to imagine a truly different way of life for themselves, let alone a totally new civilization. Of course they recognize that things are changing. But they assume today's changes will somehow pass them by. . . . They confidently expect the future to continue the present . . . a vision of a future world that is essentially "more of the same."[2]

Toffler uses the term "wave" in part to describe forms that families must take in order to cope with their new cultural environment. Economic, technological, and cultural changes come in waves, requiring families to change their structure in order to cope. While successive waves don't obliterate the old forms, they render the old way obsolete as ideal models for surviving and thriving. Toffler warned us that the families of the future would not be "more of the same," but something radically different. He saw at least three waves in history that changed family forms, the first being what he called "the extended family":

> Before the industrial revolution, for example, family forms varied from place to place. But wherever agriculture held sway, people tended to live in large, multigenerational households, with uncles, aunts, in-laws, grandparents, or cousins all living under the same roof, all working together as an economic production unit. . . . And the family was immobile — rooted to the soil.[3]

The second wave came about as American commerce became more industrialized and the family adjusted, moving from the country to the city, from the farm to the factory. Mass production, machinery, and an expanding population became the norm. And this required families to be mobile, able to pick up and follow jobs instead of staying home.

> The extended family was anything but mobile. Gradually and painfully, therefore, family structure began to change. Torn apart by the migration to the cities, battered by economic storms, families stripped themselves of unwanted relatives, grew smaller, more mobile, and more suited to the needs of the new techno-sphere.[4]

This new family was the "nuclear family": a father working outside the home, a mother working in the home, rearing a relatively small number of children.

The third wave Toffler never named, mostly because he believed that the coming culture would be so fractured that no single-family form would suffice.

> A more likely outcome is that during Third Wave civilization no single form will dominate the family mix for any long period. Instead we will see a high variety of family structures. Rather than masses of people living in uniform family arrangements, we shall see people moving through this system, tracing personalized or "customized" trajectories during the course of their lives. . . .

> This does not mean the total elimination or "death" of the nuclear family. It merely means that from now on the nuclear

family will be only one of the many socially accepted and approved forms.[5]

For Toffler, these "socially accepted and approved forms" included any conglomeration of people who found themselves mutually dependent and living under the same roof. Traditional nuclear families, blended families, single-parent families, collections of dispossessed extended kin, or even groups of friends bonding like family because they have no blood relatives could all be considered true family. Reading his work in hindsight is nothing short of amazing as twenty-first century Christians struggle to adequately answer the question, "What is a family?"

The latter part of the twentieth century brought head-spinning transformation to just about everything with the invention of the integrated circuit. Technology and its resulting affluence have created a society that, using Toffler's words, is indeed "bizarre and extreme." Parents ask questions using vocabulary unheard of twenty years ago—terms like *Internet*, *text-messaging*, and *chat room* have become commonplace. As little as ten years ago, *spam* was still canned meat. Sadly, even a "traditional" nuclear family in this century is more likely to stay in touch by putting a cell phone on each member rather than by gathering around the dinner table each night.

Popular culture and media compete to shape our values more than ever before. Video games feature levels of violence that would have earned an "R" rating for a movie made in the eighties, and horror themes, such as demons, monsters, and the occult, now rule television airwaves disguised as comedy shows targeted for teenage viewers.

Unknown Future Challenges

Every past generation worried about the unforeseen challenges waiting for the next, and rightfully so. We can be sure that one thing remains constant: *change!*

Consider the Israelite families described in the book of Exodus. The first wave was slavery in Egypt. Make bricks. Sleep through the night in exhaustion. Wake up, and head back to the mud pits. This period was Israel's first wave. Simple life. Simple family.

Then came an eighty-year-old upstart named Moses, who, after his burning-bush experience, led an exodus. Change. The Israelites were no longer slaves, but free. They were no longer settled, but wandering. Tents became their shelter instead of houses; wilderness became their scenery instead of township. A cloud by day and fire by night became their guide. They survived by eating "angel's food" that fell while they slept and drinking water from the rock. Whereas God had been silent for centuries in Egypt, He spoke regularly through Moses and Aaron and demonstrated His power through miracles. This time was a new mode of operation, a new lifestyle—their second wave. The old way of living wouldn't work in the wilderness. Their new life on the road wouldn't allow it.

But they weren't in Canaan yet, either. After a full generation—forty years—had passed, just before crossing the Jordan to experience their third wave in a "land flowing with milk and honey," Moses stopped. "Wait! Before you go in, remember the Law! I want to reiterate the Law." The book of Deuteronomy—*Deutero,* meaning "second," and *Nomos,* meaning "law"—is a reaffirmation of all God had taught them in Leviticus and Numbers.

God knew that life in Canaan would be completely different, with a whole new set of challenges that no one in Israel could predict. And He wanted to prepare them for what they were to encounter on the other side of the Jordan. Look at Moses's words:

> So the Lord commanded us to observe all these statutes, to
> fear the Lord our God *for our good always* and *for our survival* . . .
> (Deuteronomy 6:24, emphasis added)

God wanted to pass on information key to the Israelites' endurance and happiness. His purpose was not to ruin their fun or limit their freedom, but to give them a set of guidelines as they faced the immense challenge of conquering a land and settling in it. The Law was the basis of their relationship with God at that time, and He knew that a strong bond with Him would best prepare this generation to survive the changes. Throughout this reiteration of the Law in Deuteronomy, God stressed the family's role in Israel's survival.

Why God Invented the Family

Obviously, God was saying something very important about the family to Israelites more than four thousand years ago. As they were about to settle in a new land of affluence, already inhabited by idol-worshiping people, and about to begin a whole new style of living, He relied upon the family structure to preserve His covenant people. Because God preserved this ancient literature for us and we, too, face new waves of change, we had better take heed.

But why did He choose the family?

What better way to prepare the next generation for unexpected trials than by example? What better training could there be for children than watching their parents wrestle with change and still remain true to their relationship with God? It would be nice if parents could look into the future, predict specific dangers, and begin training their children to meet them. Yet Alvin Toffler did just that with uncanny accuracy in a book that saw very broad readership. If any generation had the advantage of foreknowledge, ours is the one. And still we struggle to cope. Perhaps something better is out there.

The Lord primed Israel's families for change with these words: "Watch out! Remember! Obey! Teach! Do this so you and your children will thrive." And He repeated them over and over throughout the book of Deuteronomy. The only way to prepare the next generation for unexpected trials is by living in authentic dependence upon the almighty, omniscient Creator of the Universe. This will be the mooring that keeps a family afloat as the waves of change crash around them.

Unfortunately, most of Israel's kings, and many of Judah's as well, left wicked sons and daughters to rule after them. But it doesn't have to be that way. God instituted the family as the primary means of making disciples, so as certainly as wicked kings raise delinquent children, faithful parents can guide theirs into a relationship with Jesus Christ. In fact, recent research has found that, of all professing Christians, nearly forty percent credit their family as the primary influence in their decision and that people who attended church as children are more likely to read the Bible, attend a church worship service, and pray to God during a typical week.

But, as we'll see later in this workbook, godly parents don't produce godly children automatically. A host of distractions threaten to dilute or twist the message children hear in the home, so Christian parents have to stay engaged in the process. Too many abdicate their mentoring role to Sunday school and feel that attending church regularly and praying before meals will adequately outfit their kids for spiritual battle. But what more, specifically, can they do? How can people not trained in theology or Bible teaching build a strong family that won't wash away with the next wave of change? Plenty.

Building Your Own Strong Family

We stand with Paul, who said to Timothy, "All Scripture is inspired by God and profitable for teaching, for reproof, for correction, for training in righteousness; so that the man of God may be adequate, equipped for every good work." (2 Timothy 3:16–17)

The Strong Family sermon series and *The Strong Family* workbook will lead you on a journey of personal discovery in Scripture. Together, we'll examine key passages in the Bible and draw timeless principles from them. We'll see how these principles affected the people within the narratives, what God intended the original hearers to learn, and how we can apply these principles in our time and culture.

Along the way, we'll be asking you to think about and answer questions that will:

- Draw your attention to noteworthy features in a particular passage of Scripture to help you discover for yourself what the Bible says.

- Help you see the direct connection between a passage and a principle.

- Spark your imagination to discover how you might apply a principle to your unique set of circumstances.

- Offer a relevant matter for discussion in a small group or classroom.

Our greatest desire is that when trials confront you and you find yourself without answers, your first instinct will be to ask, "I wonder what the Bible has to say about this?" You'll reach for your worn, dog-eared, marked-up copy and let the very words of God guide you. We hope that with each challenge, your children and spouse will see you turn to the only reliable source of wisdom and ultimately overcome every difficulty by your obedience to it. And we pray that by the visible transformation of your character and your ability to live well, they will want to follow in your footsteps—because they see that it *works*.

We also hope you will enjoy this time-honored, updated, and expanded lesson series, and that you will find it so valuable that you will feel confident in passing it on to your children as they begin building their own strong families.

1

AN ENDANGERED SPECIES?

Deuteronomy 6:4–15; Colossians 3:18–21

Young Elias must have hated living in the shadow of his father.

In the tumultuous years after the English Reformation, his father, the great Benjamin Keach, barely twenty-four, stood against the Crown and Parliament in defense of his beliefs. His bravery in the face of execution made him an instant hero among British Christians and, by the 1650s, his reputation as a scholar and leader earned him respect everywhere he went. Powerful in the pulpit and a tender and dedicated shepherd, he was the model pastor for over forty years. Even today, Baptists around the world recognize Benjamin Keach for influencing much of their theological heritage.

Outside the home, Keach's character was unassailable. But what did his son Elias see? Who was Benjamin Keach around the dinner table? How was the elder Keach as a father? How authentic was his spiritual life at home? The story of his son's life shows the importance of Keach's capable example.

Some described Elias as "a wild spark and a stranger to divine grace." [1] That's seventeenth-century language for "an out-of-control teenager." At nineteen, unsaved and bitter, he could no longer stand living in the Keach household and wasted no time getting as far away as he could. He boarded a ship bound for the American colonies and settled in Philadelphia—the 1687 equivalent of booking a flight into space and living on the dark side of the moon. For whatever reason, perhaps mockery, Elias passed himself off as a clergyman once he arrived.

Before long, a Baptist gathering near Philadelphia invited him to preach, and the temptation to mock his father's God was too great. He accepted. Perhaps hearing countless sermons by his father gave him enough material— and enough gall—to fake it. At any rate, the younger Keach did such a good job imitating the elder that, in the middle of the sermon, the convicting power of his own preaching became too much to bear. Trembling and frightened, he confessed everything to his hearers, asked their forgiveness, and became an authentic, believing Christian that day. Eventually, Elias became an equally effective scholar, leader, preacher, and shepherd as his father.

Church historians often remember Elias as the man who was converted under his own preaching. But is that all there was to it? The words he preached came from his father, and they led him to Jesus Christ because the Keach home put a seal of authenticity on God's Word. His father lived what he believed.

If there's one word that should describe the Christian family, it would have to be *authenticity*. In an era when genuinely godly families make the endangered species list, we can't afford not to be genuine.

Family Huddle

How real is God in your home?

To find out, ask your family the questions listed below. They're tough questions. You might not like what you hear. But the answers you receive will help you gauge your own authenticity level and give you an idea of your family's spiritual climate.

In this exercise, your purpose is not to teach or lecture, but to listen. Do your best to keep your reactions and comments to yourself. In fact, make it your goal to get other family members to talk as long as possible by asking follow-up questions that probe for more information about their perspectives and opinions. Resist the temptation to address wrongs or concerns. Your objective is to gather information, so make mental notes of the things that disturb you and plan to address them later, after prayer, reflection, and the input of godly advisors.

1. If all you knew about God came by watching me, how would you describe Him? Base your answer on:
   (a) How I relate to Him
   (b) How I solve problems and handle stress.

2. How would you describe my relationship with the Lord?

The Building Blocks: Four Essentials for Authentic Families

Let's take a look at an Old Testament blueprint for building authenticity into your home. As the Israelites prepared to enter the Promised Land, they faced an intimidating challenge—penetrating a pagan culture. Similar to the changes twenty-first century families face today, Israel was moving into a new phase. The first phase had been slavery in Egypt. The second was the wilderness wanderings. Now they were about to move into a third wave unlike anything else they had known. To prepare them for that challenge, Moses took them aside and reiterated the essentials of authentic faith—the building blocks that would help their families not only survive but also succeed.

A Permeating Love for God

For millennia, Jews have held Deuteronomy 6:4 as the quintessential declaration of their faith, a pledge of allegiance to God. They call it the *Shema* because that is the first Hebrew word in the verse. And the *Shema* is a command. "Hear!" "Listen!" "Don't miss this!" Upon rising every morning and just before going to bed the faithful Jew would recite the Shema:

> Hear, O Israel! The Lord
> is our God, the Lord is
> one! You shall love the
> Lord your God with all
> your heart and with all
> your soul and with all
> your might. These words,
> which I am commanding
> you today, shall be on
> your heart.
> (Deuteronomy 6:4–6)

By repeating this prayer, the Jewish people kept the words of God on their hearts—at the forefront of their minds. And they set an example for their families to do the same. Parents were to pass down to their children

GETTING TO THE ROOT

Deuteronomy, Moses's last words to the nation before they entered Canaan, literally means "second law" (from *deutero*, meaning "second" and *nomos*, meaning "law"). Essentially, the book is a repetition of previously revealed instructions, serving to underscore their importance. For this reason, the Ten Commandments are listed twice, once in Exodus 20 and again in Deuteronomy 5.

and grandchildren an awesome and healthy fear of God, an attentive ear to His voice, and an example of obedience to Him (Deuteronomy 6:2–3). This kind of all-encompassing love for God is authentic. You can't fake this love because the real thing oozes into every pore of one's life. Parents who model this love will forever impact their children for the better.

The Transfer of God's Truth

For authenticity to be maintained in the home, there must be a conscious, consistent transfer of God's truth to the young. First, that truth must capture the heart of the parent.

> These words, which I am commanding you today, shall be on your heart. (Deuteronomy 6:6)

Then a transfer takes place.

> You shall teach them diligently to your sons. (Deuteronomy 6:7)

Eugene Peterson renders the passage this way in *The Message*:

> Write these commandments that I've given you today on your hearts. Get them inside of you and then get them inside of your children. Talk about them wherever you are, sitting at home or walking in the street; talk about them from the time you get up in the morning to when you fall into bed at night. (Deuteronomy 6:6–7 MSG)

What exactly did Moses mean by the word *talk* used here? The Hebrew language has terms for preaching and for lecturing, but Moses used neither of these. Instead, the word used simply means "talking." No formal lecture.

GETTING TO THE ROOT

The phrase *diligently teach* comes from the Hebrew word *shanan*, meaning "to sharpen."[2] In this verse, an intensified form of the verb has been used. Moses uses it to paint a vivid word picture of someone scraping a whet stone across a blade, over and over again, until the edge is razor sharp. A dramatic but accurate translation would be, "You shall intensely sharpen your sons with these words."

No catechism. No rigid routine or Sunday school structure. And not just on Sunday or at bedtime. He simply means talking—talking that takes place naturally during all times of the day, every day. Above all else, the home should be a place where God can be comfortably discussed in any conversation, at any time.

Family Huddle

Make some time to sit with one or more members of your family and describe a time when you saw the unmistakable hand of God intervening to comfort, protect, or prosper you. Here's how to prepare ahead of time. Think through the four steps below and practice telling the story. Make it brief. Make it interesting. Make it point to the faithfulness of God.

1. Choose a very difficult or confusing time in your past, preferably one that your family members will identify with.

2. Describe the situation and how it affected you. Were you afraid, confused, angry, or lonely? In what ways did you react poorly to the situation? Be vulnerable and reveal your mistakes with only as much detail as you feel would be helpful.

3. How did God intervene? Describe the turnaround. What happened to change the bad to good?

4. Describe what the experience taught you or how it affected your relationship with God. In what ways did you become wiser, more mature, or better able to cope with life's struggles?

Bible stories are great. God gave them to us so we can learn about living in a relationship with Him by example. But He gave children parents for the very same reason. Let them read about God in the stories of your life. Then look for the transformation in theirs.

A Heart of Gratitude

Once they entered Canaan—the land of milk and honey—the Israelites experienced the same worldly temptations as we do. Suddenly, the Israelites went from wilderness paupers to, comparatively, wealthy princes. Life was no longer a Spartan diet of manna and quail, but a smorgasbord in the land of milk and honey. Canaan was like a cornucopia of fulfilled dreams: luxurious homes, sprawling estates, botanical gardens, and fertile farmland.

What is the Lord's advice for living in the midst of all this affluence? Read Deuteronomy 6:10–12, and take some time to answer the following questions.

Why do you think Moses told the people, "Then watch yourself"? What was the Lord concerned about? What was the potential cause according to the text?

_____

_____

_____

_____

_____

Do you feel as sensitive to God's presence and leading during times of adversity as you do in secure, prosperous times? Explain.

_____

_____

_____

_____

_____

"Watch out," God was saying, "So you don't forget to honor the Lord as the true source of all your blessings" (see James 1:17). An essential ingredient to keeping family faith authentic is to have a tender, humble heart of gratitude for God's provisions. Observe that God doesn't say, "Don't live in those cities," or "You shouldn't have nice things," or "You shouldn't have it so easy." He merely says, "Watch out."

Reminders of God's Faithfulness

When you're living authentic lives of faith, your children will be full of questions: What does the Bible mean? Why do we believe it? Why don't we live like others around us? You'll find that the best answers are stated reminders of God's faithfulness and grace — telling your children what God has done in your life.

Each year on Passover, thirty-five hundred years after the great Exodus from Egypt, Jewish families gather to celebrate a feast they call "the Seder." Traditionally, the youngest member of the family asks questions concerning the symbolism of the feast, and the older generations respond with the story of the Exodus. Throughout the Old Testament and still today, the Jews remember that amazing event and look to it as assurance of God's goodness and faithfulness. Similarly, His display of power in our pasts gives us confidence that His sovereignty will prevail over any evil that threatens us today.

Read Deuteronomy 6:20–24, and consider these questions:

Look at the question the son asks and the answer the Lord says to give. Based on this, list at least one purpose of the Old Testament Law.

_____

_____

_____

_____

Notice that God tells parents to rehearse God's past faithfulness to Israel and the fulfillment of His promise. How do you think this affected the children's attitude toward God and His Law?

_____

_____

_____

_____

From these verses name four things that the Lord did for Israel.

_____

_____

_____

_____

Why did God do all these things and give them the land?

_____

_____

_____

_____

Building authentic faith into our families in today's world is challenging. But help from above is available when we are obedient to God in passing on His truth to our children. God's truth is for their good . . . and for their survival.

Goal: Authentic Christian Families

Look at the commands the Lord gave the Israelite families on the brink of change: Watch out! Remember! Obey! Teach! "Do this so you and your children will thrive," He said. The way to prepare the next generation for unexpected trials is by living in authentic dependence upon the almighty, omniscient Creator of the Universe. In Deuteronomy 6, we discovered at least four essential elements of authentic dependence on God:

- A love for God that permeates the parents
- A conscious, consistent transfer of God's truth to the young
- A tender, humble heart of gratitude for God's provisions
- Frequent, stated reminders of God's faithfulness and grace

With further study, you may find even more. Cultivating these four essentials of authenticity will be difficult enough. Start by focusing on them for the next couple of weeks, with the goal to have them become unconscious characteristics of your family. Fortunately, you aren't alone. What God ordains, He sustains. Invite Him to make these a part of your daily life, and allow His power to accomplish what you can't. He won't let you down. Just look at His track record.

2

Masculine Model of Leadership
1 Thessalonians 2:8–12

In his book *Promises to Peter: Building a Bridge from Parent to Child*, Charlie Shedd tells how the title of his sermon on parenting reflected his changing experiences as a father. Before he was a father, he called this sermon "How to Raise Your Children." People came in droves to hear it. After one child, he waited awhile before preaching "Some Suggestions to Parents." Two more children and he was calling it "Feeble Hints to Fellow Strugglers." Several more years and children later, he seldom gave that sermon. But when he did, his theme was "Anyone Here Got a Few Words of Wisdom?"

Being a dad is tough. Living up to your own standards is hard enough, to say nothing of meeting God's standards. And the toughest part of all is that deep inside, every father knows he is leaving an indelible thumbprint on the life of each of his children. Whether he's nuts-and-bolts practical or scrapes the Milky Way with his visionary ideas; whether he's strong and aggressive or weak and passive; whether he's a workaholic or an alcoholic—every dad knows that his influence will mold and shape his children into the adults they become.

How can fathers do this carefully and wisely? In this chapter we will take a few tips on parenting from the apostle Paul's letter to the Thessalonians, his children in the faith.

A Little Background

The first two European churches Paul founded were in Philippi and Thessalonica. When he traveled to Thessalonica, he saw potential in that city and wanted to stay, even though he was pursued and persecuted by unbelievers (see 1 Thessalonians 2:1–2). For six weeks, he poured himself into a handful of believers there, working night and day to establish them in their newborn faith. Although Paul never returned for another extended visit, the Thessalonian believers had captured his heart. So when he later heard about the waves of persecution that threatened to drown their belief, he threw them two life preservers: he sent Timothy to them (1 Thessalonians 3:2) and he wrote them a letter. Pouring through his pen was a wellspring of love from a father's heart. He wrote:

> We proved to be gentle among you, as a nursing mother tenderly cares for her own children. . . . exhorting and encouraging and imploring each one of you as a father would his own children. (1 Thessalonians 2:7, 11)

The words "as a . . . mother . . . as a father" appear nowhere else in Paul's writings. The imagery implies tenderness, compassion, protection, and instruction.

Why do you think Paul chose the roles of mother and father to picture his relationship with the Thessalonian believers?

_____

_____

_____

_____

What do Paul's relationship with the Thessalonians and your relationship with your children have in common?

_____

_____

_____

_____

Five Guidelines for Dads

From Paul's parental language in 1 Thessalonians 2:8–12, we can paint an instructive portrait of a dad with his kids. Let's look at the vivid colors and subtle strokes that make this portrait so striking. We'll consider five essential guidelines for dads: demonstrating a fond affection, leading a transparent life, exhibiting unselfish diligence, cultivating spiritual authenticity, and being a positive influence.

Demonstrate a Fond Affection

As we look at Paul's life with his spiritual children, the first quality we see is affection:

> Having so fond an affection for you . . . (1 Thessalonians 2:8)

Paul made sure the Thessalonians knew of his deep love for them, his "children" in the faith.

Why do you think it was important to Paul that the Thessalonians knew of his affection for them?

_____

_____

_____

What influence did this likely have on their view of Paul's instruction?

_____

_____

_____

_____

How often do we express to our children the kind of fond affection Paul talks about? Hugging and kissing a baby or a small child is easy—they're likely to hug and kiss you back! But as that child grows up, physical affection is often replaced with physical aloofness, which can have disastrous results.

Research reveals that if a child is to become a well-adjusted adult capable of healthy relationships and wise life-choices, physical affection from his or her dad is essential. In fact, one study revealed that promiscuous women shared at least one common factor: homes where the father had been unaffectionate.[3] Appropriate nonverbal communication of closeness, touching,

GETTING TO THE ROOT

The term *affection* means "to feel one's self drawn to something or someone."[1] Another popular dictionary describes it as having "a strong feeling intensified by an inner attachment."[2] The image is both masculine and tender. It describes a picture of a father who feels affectionately drawn to his child. He wants to hold his little one close, and when he's away, he can't wait to feel those little arms around his neck again.

and kissing conveys the message, "I appreciate you. I'm so very proud of you. You mean so much to me."

Think about your children for a moment. If they had only physical, nonverbal communication to go by, what message do you think they would receive from you?

_____

_____

_____

_____

Lead a Transparent Life

The rest of 1 Thessalonians 2:8 reveals the second guideline for dads to follow: lead a transparent life.

> Having so fond an affection for you, we were well-pleased to impart to you not only the gospel of God but *also our own lives*, because you had become very dear to us. (1 Thessalonians 2:8, emphasis added)

Isn't the gospel important? Absolutely! And isn't it enough? Absolutely not!

Your children must hear the gospel if they are to come to know the Savior you love; it'll ring even more true if the good news comes from your own lips. But they need more than that. They need instruction about life, and they need a father who demonstrates how to live a godly life—mistakes and all. They need to see how you make decisions, what your values are, how you handle your finances, and what makes you laugh. They need to hear you admit when you're wrong and see you stand up for your faith. They need to know you inside out—and to feel your interest and belief in them. The word *impart* means "to convey, to contribute, to share fully" . . . with children who know without a doubt that they are "very dear" to you.

How comfortable do you feel letting your children see your imperfections?

_____

_____

_____

_____

If you let them see your struggle to be a good parent, employee, friend, or Christian, what effect do you think it would have on them?

_____

_____

_____

_____

Exhibit an Unselfish Diligence

In 1 Thessalonians 2:9, we see Paul hard at work, making sacrifices for the sake of Christ.

> For you recall, brethren, our labor and hardship, how working night and day so as not to be a burden to any of you, we proclaimed to you the gospel of God.

Another mark of a great father is hard work—diligence. Paul was dedicated to providing for himself so he could relieve his disciples of any responsibility to care for him. He expected that demonstrating solid, strong, and consistent commitment to work would speak as loudly as his words.

Similarly, a loving father will do whatever he must to protect and provide for his family. Richard Halverson dedicated his book *Perspective: Devotional Thoughts for Men* to "faithful Christian laymen who with silent heroism under relentless secular pressure fight the economic battle as stewards of the living God." He added, "Thank God upon every remembrance of these faithful men."[4] By being good stewards of the living God, fathers can demonstrate to their kids that all material blessings are from the hand of God. They can teach generosity, unselfishness, and wisdom by giving rather than hoarding and by saving rather than spending rashly.

Families don't need material blessing at the expense of Dad's presence, but they do need to see him exhibit discipline, determination, and devotion to making their world secure. And a father can only pass along those qualities by example. A hardworking father can help his children discover what motivates him and what spurs him on to get the job done, even when the task is unpleasant or hampered by difficulty.

On the other hand, men can find it easy to provide material things in place of giving themselves. Not only does this rob children of the opportunity to enjoy their father, they also may come to despise what they had no stake in obtaining.

Cultivate Spiritual Authenticity

Two important aspects of a father's responsibility to cultivate authenticity are belief and behavior.

> We proclaimed to you the gospel of God. You are witnesses, and so is God, how devoutly and uprightly and blamelessly we behaved toward you believers. (1 Thessalonians 2:9–10)

These verses disclose what Paul did to influence the Thessalonians when he was with them. "We proclaimed" (v. 9) and "we behaved" (v. 10). Paul revealed his ultimate desire for the Thessalonian believers later in chapter 2, verse 12: "so that you would walk in a manner worthy of the God who calls you." See the connection? Paul was saying, "When I was with you, I proclaimed to you the good news. I gave you the truth. But I also demonstrated the power of that truth by my behavior, so that you could grow."

Don't worry, though. Spiritual authenticity doesn't presume to be perfect. How well a father lives out his spiritual belief is certainly important, but far more crucial is how well he tries. And so we find the basis of spiritual leadership in the home: leading by trying, failing, adjusting, and trying again, and steadily growing in obedience every day.

If a boss or someone with authority over you were to talk one way and live another way, what would be your opinion of them?

_____

_____

_____

_____

How do you think it would affect your willingness to follow their leadership?

_____

_____

_____

_____

Be a Positive Influence

The final stroke on our painting of parenthood is to be a positive influence, a trait Paul exhibited toward the Thessalonians.

> You know how we were exhorting and encouraging and imploring each one of you as a father would his own children, so that you would walk in a manner worthy of the God who calls you into His own kingdom and glory. (1 Thessalonians 2:11–12)

Have you ever needed advice and motivation to complete a difficult task? Thinking back, what could someone have done to help you?

_____

_____

_____

_____

GETTING TO THE ROOT

The term translated "exhorting" is the Greek word *parakaleo*; the same word used of the Holy Spirit, who is often called the *Paraclete*. Think of a coach running alongside an athlete in a long-distance race, giving him split times and information about the other runners, feedback on his performance, strategy given his current situation, and, perhaps, something to motivate him to dig deep and try harder. That's a *paraclete*. That's Paul's positive influence in Thessalonica. That's a father's way of helping his kids succeed.

Let's examine the ways Paul positively influenced his spiritual children—the ways he "encouraged" and "implored" them as a father would.

You may be surprised that the kind of encouragement Paul talked about involves much more than cheering at a soccer game or applauding at a concert. The word *encourage* comes from a word used only three other times in the New Testament—once later in 1 Thessalonians, and twice by John. In John's gospel, Mary and Martha mourned the loss of their brother, Lazarus, so their neighbors gathered to *console* them. Paul uses this same word. Loving fathers have open, welcoming arms. Their hearts ache for their children when they suffer. And, rather than lecture, loving fathers identify with their children's pain and give them hope for better times. This kind of encouragement lifts the spirit and restores the soul.

Can you think of a time when someone close to you has suffered a loss, or struggled against a hardship? What did you do to make the situation more bearable?

_____

_____

_____

_____

Imploring comes from the same word we use for *martyr*. Martyrs don't merely speak the truth, they implore others to accept it by enduring pain and even death. By their suffering, they influence others to take the message seriously and to join them in living it out.

Is there a message or a perspective you feel is crucial for your children to take as their own? What are you willing to suffer or sacrifice in order for them to understand and embrace it?

_____

_____

_____

_____

In this last characteristic of a loving father (Be a Positive Influence) the emphasis is on the word *positive*. Rarely do negative messages inspire people to greatness. But, for some reason, being negative comes easier to us, and we have to be deliberate about being positive. In fact, Dan Benson, in his book *The Total Man*, tells us the results of a disturbing survey: For every single positive statement made in the average home, there are ten negative ones.[5] Being positive while your kids are maturing is difficult. Part of your job is correcting them, right? But children whose ears are full of the words like "No!" and "Don't!" and "Stop that!" learn not to trust their instincts . . . not to try. Children who hear "That's great!" and "You can do it!" as often as they hear "That's not a good idea," will face new challenges with self-confidence and explore their potential without fear.

Family Huddle

Make some time to talk with each of your family members one-on-one, and ask them this question:

What's one thing you've always wanted to try doing, but felt it might be silly, weird, or too risky?

Be prepared to accept any answer. The dream may be as wild as skydiving, or as simple as trying a new restaurant. Whatever the response, the point is to be receptive and positive; you'll find enough time to be realistic later. Join them in the dream. Combine your imaginations and have fun with it. And, if possible, see if you can make that dream happen—together.

Just look at all the possibilities that surround you. At one time, those were impossibilities, until someone dared to stretch his or her imagination and wonder, "What if?" Teach your family how to be can-do people by teaching them how to dream.

Again, the five guidelines for being the type of dad we found in 1 Thessalonians 2:8–12 are:

- Demonstrate a fond affection

- Lead a transparent life

- Exhibit an unselfish diligence

- Cultivate spiritual authenticity

- Be a positive influence

The role of being a father is incredibly challenging and takes lots of work. The sacrifices required frighten most men such that they either avoid the role altogether or abandon it to others. Yet, a father's godly influence plays an indispensable part in the development of healthy, wise, and self-sustaining adults. Godly influence is essential! And only eternity can measure the rewards.

3

POSITIVE PARTNER OF SUPPORT
Selected Scriptures

Perhaps no other role has undergone more redefinition in the last half-century than the role of mothers. The fifties and sixties celebrated moms with perhaps too much idealism. In the seventies, many feminists considered full-time motherhood to be a parasitic existence that degraded women. By the eighties the rhetoric had eased a bit, but mothers who devoted all their time to childcare still bore the brand of being "lazy." The nineties celebrated the beleaguered but victorious I-can-have-it-all career mother. By the turn of the century, many of these career supermoms discovered how much they were missing and set aside some of their professional aspirations to become one of the millions of "soccer moms" that dominated the social and political landscape.

Today, go to a PTA meeting in most any school and you're likely to see a business-suited career mother, an arts-and-crafts homemaker, and an SUV-driving soccer mom swapping "war stories" like no difference exists between them. No matter how motherhood may look in the political arena or in sociology textbooks, mothers are all the same when you put a child in their arms. In this chapter, we'll discover from Scripture at least five qualities of a great mom. But first, let's get back to basics. What does it take to create and manage a God-centered home life?

A Firm Foundation

All homes must be built on a firm foundation. In Proverbs 24:3–4 we see the tools needed to establish a rock-solid home.

> By *wisdom* a house is built,
> And by *understanding* it is established;
> And by *knowledge* the rooms are filled
> With all precious and pleasant riches. (emphasis added)

Solomon suggested that homes are built with three primary tools: wisdom, understanding, and knowledge. Wisdom is the ability to see with discernment—to view life through God's eyes. Understanding is the skill of responding with insight—reading between the lines. Knowledge is learning with perception—having a teachable spirit and a willingness to learn . . . even from our children.

These tools have nothing to do with hammer and nails or trowel and mortar. The tools Solomon describes are relational. Moms, you can have all three. Using God-given wisdom, understanding, and knowledge, you can fill the rooms of your home with a rich heritage of godly character traits, deep relationships, and lasting memories. So, just what does this process look like in the real world? Let's take a look at one New Testament example.

A New Testament Example

The New Testament shows us how Timothy's mother molded her son's spiritual heritage by using the tools of wisdom, understanding, and knowledge. Although we don't know much about Timothy's mother, we can learn about her spiritual life from the legacy she and her mother, Timothy's grandmother, passed down to him. The apostle Paul recognized this when he wrote to Timothy: "For I am mindful of the sincere faith within you, which first dwelt in your grandmother Lois and your mother Eunice, and I am sure that it is in you as well" (2 Timothy 1:5).

Paul appreciated the honest faith he saw in Timothy and was drawn to him, forging a fifteen-year friendship. As Paul lay dying in a Roman dungeon, Timothy was the friend he sought out.

> Paul . . . to Timothy, my beloved son. . . . I thank God, whom I serve with a clear conscience the way my forefathers did, as I constantly remember you in my prayers night and day, longing to see you, even as I recall your tears, so that I may be filled with joy. (2 Timothy 1:1–4)

Looking back on their friendship, Paul was filled with gratitude and good memories. In the verses that follow, we'll discover the qualities that made Timothy unique and appealing—qualities he learned from his mother.

A Mother's Contributions

In 2 Timothy 1:4–7 we find five distinct contributions a mother can make to the family, filling each room with her motherly touch until her house becomes a home.

Transparent Tenderness

Paul first mentions Timothy's tears:

> Even as I recall your tears,
> so that I may be filled with joy.
> (2 Timothy 1:4)

> ### In Other Words
>
> It is a wise adult who understands that self-esteem is the most fragile characteristic in human nature, and once broken, its reconstruction is more difficult than repairing Humpty Dumpty.[1]
>
> —Dr. James Dobson

Paul remembered Timothy's tenderness, a trait likely passed down from his mother. In fact, many of us learned tenderness from our mothers, while our dads taught us diligence. From Dad we likely learned the value of a dollar and the importance of standing alone when everything turns against us. And we more than likely learned transparent tenderness from Mom.

Mothers, don't lose that quality—your tenderness is one of your greatest contributions to your family. Your warm embrace, eager smile, and soft reply will be a safe harbor for the child who has been tossed and battered by life's stormy seas.

Think about your own mother or a person who had a significant motherly influence on you and describe a time you saw her tenderness on display.

_____

_____

_____

_____

Many times "tough love" may be the best approach, but at other times, tenderness may be a better response. Describe a time in your life when someone's compassion would have comforted you.

_____

_____

_____

If you have a child, describe a time he or she needed your tears or deep compassion. How did you respond? What effect do you think it had on your relationship?

GETTING TO THE ROOT

The New American Standard Bible translates the phrase *honest faith* in 2 Timothy 1:5 as "sincere faith." The word translated "sincere" comes from the Greek term, *anhupocritos.* You can probably see the English word *hypocrite* hiding in there. The *an* tacked on to the front negates it. *Non-hypocritical* is barely adequate, though. Other words make better sense of what a Greek writer would have had in mind; words like *genuine, honest, open, straightforward,* or *sincere* are closer to the intended meaning. The very best English word would have to be *authentic.*

Authentic Spirituality

As we have already seen in 2 Timothy 1:5, Paul referred directly to Timothy's spiritual heritage, his roots:

> That precious memory triggers another: your honest faith—and what a rich faith it is, handed down from your grand-mother Lois to your mother Eunice, and now to you! (MSG)

The genuineness of Timothy's faith made him so famous among the men in towns sixty miles away that when Paul passed through the region, he had to see this remarkable man for himself (see Acts 16:1–5). The Apostle saw in Timothy the same authentic brand of spirituality that he saw in Lois and Eunice, and he wanted Timothy to join him in his mission.

Inner Confidence

> For this reason I remind you to kindle afresh the gift of God which is in you through the laying on of my hands. For God has not given us a spirit of timidity, but of *power* and love and discipline. (2 Timothy 1:6–7, emphasis added)

Notice that timidity is not a desirable trait—it's a synonym for insecurity or inferiority. If you possess a timid spirit, you'll be amazed to see your children sense your attitude toward yourself—and to see them emulate it, whether in good or bad ways. One reason Timothy stayed true to the Scriptures and stood strong in his ministry was that he had learned inner confidence from his mother. Moms, do you know that God wants to use you to build healthy self-esteem in your child?

And just how do you do that? Consider this:

GETTING TO THE ROOT

The word *power* used in 2 Timothy 1:6–7 comes from the Greek term *dunamis.* You may have heard preachers say that we get the word *dynamite* from *dunamis* and, strictly speaking, that's true. The Swedish inventor Alfred Nobel did borrow from the Greek dictionary to name his new product, but it makes for poor imagery.

Dunamis probably comes from the Greek verb *dunasthai,* meaning "to be able." A better picture of this would be an engine. *Dunamis* has in mind an inherent strength, an inner might, a raw ability to translate potential into action. *Dunamis* power isn't explosive; it's steady, controlled, purposeful, and always ready.

Although our task is more difficult for some children than for others, there are ways to teach a child of his genuine significance, regardless of the shape of his nose or the size of his ears or the efficiency of his mind. Every child is entitled to hold up his head, not in haughtiness and pride, but in confidence and security. This is the concept of human worth intended by our Creator. How foolish for us to doubt our value when He formed us in His own image! . . .

. . . When the child is convinced that he is greatly loved and respected by his parents, he is inclined to accept his own worth as a person.[2]

Inner confidence, like transparent tenderness and authentic spirituality, is passed down from generation to generation . . . in Timothy's life, it passed from grandmother to mother to son.

Have you ever seen your mother fight an injustice, defend an underdog, or take up a hopeless moral cause based on principle? Describe her actions in a couple of sentences. What effect did it have on you?

_____

_____

_____

_____

When was the last time you showed moral courage in front of your children? Did you take time to explain what you were doing? How do you think they will be different as a result?

_____

_____

_____

_____

Are your children timid? Being timid is not the same as being shy. Timidity comes from fear and a general lack of confidence in one's ability to meet difficulty head-on. Based on our study so far, how can you help your children find the strength they need to enjoy life?

_____

_____

_____

_____

Unselfish Love

Second Timothy 1:7 continues with another gift from God—a gift everyone, especially mothers, can emulate: _love._

> For God has not given us a spirit of timidity, but of power
> and _love._ (emphasis added)

We use the word _love_ all the time, but what does it really look like? Real love is displayed through action. Put transparent tenderness, authentic spirituality, moral courage, and unselfish love together and you know what you get? Someone like Catherine Lawes.

Catherine Lawes was a young mother of three small children when her husband, Lewis, became the warden at New York's Sing Sing Prison in 1921. No other prison in America came close to the toughness of Sing Sing in those days, and everyone warned her from the beginning that she should never set foot inside its walls. But that didn't stop Catherine. When the prison held its first basketball game, in she went with her three children and sat right up there in the stands with the inmates. As far as safety was concerned, her attitude was: "My husband and I are going to take care of these men, and I believe they will take care of me! I don't have to worry!"

Her desire to know the men had her studying their records. When she discovered that one convicted murderer was blind, she taught him how to read braille. When she encountered an inmate who was deaf, she went to school to learn sign language.

After years of this kind of faithful, unselfish love, Catherine died in an auto accident. The whole prison instinctively felt it even before hearing the announcement. As her body lay in a casket in her home three-quarters of a mile from the prison, the toughest, most hardened criminals in America gathered at the front gate and wept. Men that goodness had forgotten grieved the loss of a mother's love. The acting warden opened the prison gate and said, "Alright, men, you can go. Just be sure and check in tonight!" A parade of criminals walked without a guard the three-quarters of a mile to the Lawes' home to say good-bye to Catherine. And every one of them checked back in.

By the time Warden Lawes retired, Sing Sing had become a humanitarian institution. When asked about the transformation, he said, "I owe it all to my wonderful wife, Catherine, who is buried outside the prison walls."[3]

The life of Catherine Lawes gives us a picture of the fourth essential quality that mothers bring to their family: unselfish love. Paul used the word *agapē* to indicate seeking the highest, best good of another person. *Agapē* finds its motivation in the seat of the will. It may be combined with romantic love for a mate or the warm affection for a friend, but warm feelings are not a prerequisite for the exercise of *agapē*. *Agapē* chooses to love the unlovely, and it almost always involves sacrifice. "But God demonstrates His own love [*agapē*] toward us, in that while we were yet sinners, Christ died for us" (Romans 5:8).

Self-control

Take a final look at 2 Timothy 1:7.

> For God did not give us a spirit of timidity, but a spirit of power, of love and of *self-discipline*. (NIV, emphasis added)

Purposeful moms balance tenderness and love with discipline. They set parameters and know when it's time to say, "That's it; that's enough." In his book *Hide or Seek*, James Dobson tells the story of a research project conducted by Dr. Stanley Coopersmith, associate professor of psychology at the University of California. After studying 1,738 middle-class boys and their families over a number of years, Coopersmith identified three important differences between the family lives of boys with high self-esteem and of those with low self-worth.

First, the children with high esteem were more loved and appreciated at home. Their parents' love was deep and real; the words they spoke to their children had substance.

Second, and perhaps most revealing, the group with high esteem had parents whose approach to discipline was significantly stricter. They taught self-control. In contrast, the parents of the low-esteem group were much more permissive, which created a sense of insecurity. These boys were more likely to feel that no one cared enough to enforce the rules.

Third, the high-esteem group had homes that were characterized by democracy and open communication. Once boundaries had been established, the boys had the freedom to ask questions and express themselves in an environment of acceptance.[4]

Moms, don't underestimate the value of teaching self-control. In your discipline, you are building your children's character, enhancing their self-esteem, and helping them learn to be responsible for themselves.

 Family Huddle

If you're a mother, use the chart below to evaluate and rate how you're doing. Don't worry! No one will score a 5 on every trait, and no one deserves a 1 on all of them either. Take some time with this and ask God to help you be realistic, but fair. Look at it several times over a one-week period to make sure your mood doesn't overly influence your evaluation. Mark the chart using three different colors of pen:

Use a RED pen to rate how well you exhibit each trait.
Use a BLUE pen to indicate how well your mother exhibited it.
Use a BLACK pen to gauge how well your family reflects each trait.

Character Trait	Poor			Fair	Excellent
Transparent tenderness	1	2	3	4	5
Authentic spirituality	1	2	3	4	5
Inner confidence	1	2	3	4	5
Unselfish love	1	2	3	4	5
Self-control	1	2	3	4	5

Do you see any patterns? Any inherited strengths or weaknesses? Do you notice any important traits that you aren't passing on to your children?

A Return to Our Foundation

How do mothers build homes with solid values? They first secure the foundation. Remember the tools?

> By *wisdom* a house is built,
> And by *understanding* it is established;
> And by *knowledge* the rooms are filled
> With all precious and pleasant riches.
> (Proverbs 24:3–4, emphasis added)

The riches that fill the rooms of a godly home are transparent tenderness, authentic spirituality, inner confidence, unselfish love, and self-control. Children see what God's love is all about through their parents—especially their mothers, since they often spend the most time with them.

You may have noticed that these qualities are as much Christlike as motherly. Describe how your personal spiritual walk currently affects your role as a mother.

_____

_____

_____

_____

What are some specific ways your spouse (or other significant individual, if you're single) can support you as you develop the qualities that will make you a better mom? Or, if you are in a position to encourage a mother, name some specific ways you can support her.

_____

_____

_____

The Image of God in a Mother's Love

Mel Gibson's movie, *The Passion of the Christ*, includes a number of scenes and details that don't appear in Scripture. The filmmaker's personal touches often add richness to the telling of Christ's agonizing death experience and, without changing the theology, give us perspectives we may not have considered.

In one scene, Jesus's mother sees Him crash to the pavement beneath the burden of His cross and the soldiers' beating. Memories of His childhood rush to her mind. She remembers Jesus falling to the ground, as all boys do, and her rushing to pick Him up. Now she can do nothing to help Him.

Every mother watching felt Mary's anguish. In the movie she portrayed the quintessential mother: indomitable, magnificent, strong, stable, ever-present. Through her, we see something of God's anguish as He watched His Son suffer.

Mel Gibson did in his movie the same thing that God did for us in life. He gave us examples of motherly love to let us know what His love is all about. When you see a mother swell with emotion, you see Him. When you hear her cry, you hear Him cry. Every swat on the behind, every consoling hug, every cheer from the stands bears His seal of authenticity. In a mother, we see the likeness of the Creator—the marvelous, matchless mother-love of a Father God.

4

YOUR BABY HAS THE BENTS (PART ONE)
Proverbs 22:6

Often parents view the cooing bundle they bring home from the maternity ward as a cuddly lump of clay, soft and completely pliable in their hands. They believe they can take the personality of their baby, squeeze it, roll it, mold it into any shape they desire, pop it into a kiln until it's good and hard, and send it out to face the world.

But that perception of child rearing fails to take into account the inherent properties of the clay itself. Those characteristics determine, to a large extent, how it can be shaped and how it will respond to the kiln. Likewise, although the hands of the parent can influence the personality of the child, the preestablished characteristics of the child determine how and to what extent it can be molded.

In this lesson we'll take a look at Proverbs 22:6, a key passage in discovering and developing those inborn characteristics.

> Train up a child in the way he should go,
> Even when he is old he will not depart from it.

As integral as this verse is to raising children, few parents understand what it really says.

The Popular Interpretation of Proverbs 22:6

Many see this verse as saying that if children have been carted off to church every Sunday, made to read the Bible each day, instructed to memorize Scripture, and taught to read only Christian books and see only Christian films, then those children will stay on the appropriate path. And, even if they do play the prodigal and journey into some distant country morally, at some point they will come to their senses and get back on course.

As popular as this interpretation is, it doesn't always square with experience. Real life teaches us that not all prodigals come home. The bottom of the ocean is strewn with the wreckage of ships that have strayed from their course and never returned safely to harbor.

Sadly, our memories, too, are strewn with the shipwrecked lives of loved ones who charted courses onto the high seas, rode immorality's crest, and sank.

The Proper Interpretation of Proverbs 22:6

Not only does the popular interpretation of Proverbs 22:6 fall short experientially, but as we examine the verse, we quickly see that the popular interpretation isn't what the writer intended to communicate.

The Nature of the Training

"Train up" comes from the Hebrew verb *hanakh*, which means "to dedicate, or consecrate."[1] Israelites used it to commission buildings and altars for a specific purpose. That's great for buildings and presidents, but what about children? Surely God doesn't expect us to have an infant raise a tiny hand and swear an oath! No, the perspective Scripture says we are to have is one in which we dedicate them—and ourselves—to a specific purpose. But the word *hanakh* has much more to teach us.

Many Hebrew verbs have a close association with a picturesque noun. In this case, "inaugurate" or "train up" comes from a word that refers to the roof of the mouth or the gums.[2] An ancient custom helps us understand what seems to be an odd connection.

As many new mothers know, some babies will cry for their mother's milk but don't know how to nurse. Midwives in the East learned to overcome the problem by massaging the infant's gums and palate with the tart juices of crushed dates or grapes before nursing. This encouraged behavior that both relieved the mother and gave the baby exactly what he needed. Likewise, parents are to create a thirst within their children for gaining wisdom and knowledge.

The Duration of the Training

In Proverbs 22:6, the word *child* (in "train up a child") generally calls to mind a little one somewhere between infancy and four or five years of age. However, the Scriptures use this term in a broader sense, ranging anywhere from a newborn to a person of marriageable age. Although translated differently at times, the same Hebrew word for *child* is used in many different passages. For example, in 1 Samuel 4:21 the term *boy* is used to describe a newborn. In Exodus 2:3 *child* is used to describe three-month-old Moses. In 1 Samuel 1:22 *child* is used to portray Samuel before he was weaned. In Genesis 21:12, 17–20 *lad* is used to refer to Ishmael, a preteen. In Genesis 37:2 *youth* is used of Joseph at age seventeen. And in Genesis 34:19 *young man* is used for someone of marriageable age. The point is that the principle in Proverbs 22:6 applies to any dependent child still living under the parents' roof.

The Implementation of the Training

"In the way he should go" is probably the most debated phrase in the proverb. The Hebrew is quite simply "in accordance with his way" (or even more literally, "into the mouth of his way"), so translating this phrase is anything but simple. Some suggest that "in the book of Proverbs there are only two ways that a person can go: the way of the wise or [the way of] righteousness, and the way of the fool."[3] And, in a broad sense, that's right. But the writer's artful use of language tells us that his advice goes far beyond the obvious.

The key Hebrew word in the phrase is *derek*, meaning "way." It can refer to a literal way, such as a road, or it can be less literal, referring to the manner in which something acts, as in Proverbs 30:18–19:

> There are three things which are too wonderful for me,
> Four which I do not understand:
> The *way* of an eagle in the sky,
> The *way* of a serpent on a rock,
> The *way* of a ship in the middle of the sea,
> And the *way* of a man with a maid (emphasis added).

The most colorful use of *derek* has to do with stringing an archer's bow, which in Solomon's time was a piece of wood with a natural curve to it—a natural bent. In Psalm 7:12 the word is used of God, who "has bent His bow and made it ready." God has set His foot on the bow in order to bend it and string it. The bow's bend and the string's tension give an arrow the power of flight. In a similar way, God puts His foot on the physical, psychological, and personality bows of our lives to bend them in specific ways to accomplish a specific purpose.

Think about your siblings or friends you knew growing up. How were they similar?

_____

_____

_____

_____

How were they different?

_____

_____

_____

_____

Which were more obvious, their similarities or their differences? How did these characteristics affect their choice of occupation, their choice of mate, or what kind of family they decided to have?

_____

_____

_____

_____

As parents, we must be careful to avoid two errors: first, rearing our children exactly the way we were reared—mistakes and all; and second, comparing our children with each other and applying the same approach to all. Both errors stem from a failure to understand and appreciate how marvelously each child is made.

The Results of the Training

The latter portion of Proverbs 22:6 states that "when he is old he will not depart from it." The root meaning of the Hebrew word for *old* is "hair on the chin." It suggests someone approaching adulthood, not retirement. Solomon is not envisioning a sixty-year-old prodigal returning home. He's thinking of a boy who's just starting to grow a beard. Thus, when the child reaches maturity, he will not depart from the way in which he has been trained.

The Parental Application of Proverbs 22:6

Children often become angry and bitter on their own, even in the best homes with the best parents. But more often kids rebel because of parental insensitivity—being too involved in other things to slow down and know their children or trying to raise their children the way they were raised. But Scripture says that every child is different. Before parents can guide a child in "his way," they have to know the child.

But how can a parent, a mere human, hope to truly know his or her child's heart? Scripture says the best way to know a child is to observe his or her conduct. "It is by his deeds that a lad distinguishes himself / If his conduct is pure and right. / The hearing ear and the seeing eye, the Lord has made both of them" (Proverbs 20:11–12). God can see directly into each person's soul and determine exactly how he or she should be trained. Ask God to give you a sensitive spirit and to help you learn to be deliberate as you study your child.

Family Huddle

Can you imagine how hard it would be to play a game in which the rules changed without notice? Just when you have it figured out and have some hope that you might win, the very things that helped you get ahead suddenly put you behind. With enough of that kind of exasperation, you'd probably be tempted to quit.

You and your spouse come from different households and may have grown up with two very different child-rearing styles. These styles may be compatible, and they may not. Without examining them, you may be putting your children in a no-win situation. They may either quit trying to learn the game or they may simply rebel.

Take some time with your spouse to reflect on how your parents raised each of you and how that influences your current approach. Are the two of you giving your children a consistent set of rules for the game of life? Some questions are listed below to help you get started. Remember, the key is to listen and understand your spouse.

1. Was your home very strict or a let-it-all-hang-out kind of place? Describe what growing up was like in your parents' home.

2. Were your parents' expectations for you high, non-existent, or somewhere in between? How were their expectations communicated to you?

3. No parent is perfect. Think of some particular child-rearing mistakes your parents made that you want to avoid with your children.

4. Identifying mistakes is easy. Finding solutions can be much more difficult. With each mistake you listed, consider how you plan to keep from repeating that error.

5. Describe how you were disciplined and how that affects your view of discipline.

6. Compare and contrast your experience with that of your spouse. Discuss how each of you can adjust your approach to give your children a consistent set of expectations, rules, and consequences to live and learn by.

Your children are making themselves known. The question is, are you noticing? If you're beginning to feel that you don't really know or understand them, now is the best time to start. Thinking about each child separately, answer these questions:

Is your son or daughter self-disciplined and studious, or artistic and impulsive? How does this affect his or her performance in school?

_____

_____

_____

_____

How can you work with teachers to take advantage of your child's natural bent?

_____

_____

_____

_____

How are you and your child alike? How are you different? In what way does this affect the way you guide him or her?

_____

_____

_____

_____

How does your child respond to being punished? Does your discipline have the desired effect, or does it seem to make the problem worse? If you feel that your methods of discipline aren't working, can you think of some other method or style that would result in behavior that would make you both happy?

_____

_____

_____

_____

Seabiscuit, the champion race horse, was terribly difficult to train. First, his trainers had so mismanaged his natural bents that they had created in him an obstinate spirit that resisted instruction. Second, he was unlike any other horse on the track. For instance, Seabiscuit loved to stay close to the rail, which was the worst part of the track, and would run his fastest only there. In addition, he fought any rider who pulled back on the reins to slow him down. Where others saw obstinacy, Tom Smith saw heart. Where "by-the-book" trainers saw quirks, Smith saw opportunity. When Smith and his trainers couldn't break Seabiscuit of these habits, they used them to their advantage. "Smith told his riders to adjust the horse's speed with steering. When a rider wanted Seabiscuit to speed up, he would swing him toward the rail; when he wanted him to ease off, he'd nudge him to the outside."[4]

In training Seabiscuit, Smith used conventional wisdom where it worked and ignored it where appropriate. Because he knew that horses had been created with a purpose, and he knew his horse's distinctive behavioral traits, the trainer judged every method by one question: "Will it make Seabiscuit want to run faster?"

The single most significant contribution you can make to your child is to know your child. What works for every other parent may not help your children at all. God created each child with a unique bent, and to fight it is to fight God's creation. Instead, learn who your children are by developing an intimate relationship with each one. Ask God to help you make the most of your child's natural tendencies to best live in harmony with God's design. Help each child discover his or her road—the unique path he or she should follow. When maturity comes, their success will be a legacy you can enjoy together.

5

YOUR BABY HAS THE BENTS (PART TWO)
Proverbs 22:6; Psalm 139

Edwin and John were the sons of Junius Brutus Booth, a brilliant actor who came to the United States in 1821 and quickly made the Booth name synonymous with great theater.

Edwin started early, debuting in *Richard III* at the tender age of fifteen, opposite his father. At first, critics felt certain that the great Booth talent had overlooked the boy. But he worked hard and studied on his own in California, Australia, and the Sandwich Islands. Soon reports about his brilliant performances made their way back to the East Coast. By the time Junius died, Edwin had earned the respect of the theater elite in New York and London, and soon his fame eclipsed his father's.

John displayed considerable skill on the stage, but many said his lack of confidence and certain eccentricities would forever keep stardom out of reach. Perhaps these problems surfaced because politics and intrigue held greater fascination for him. In November of 1864, Booth met with a group of conspirators to devise a plan to kidnap President Lincoln and bargain for the release of Confederate prisoners of war. The attempt failed. Less than a month later, John acted on his own, stole onto America's political stage, and fired a bullet into Abraham Lincoln's head in Ford's Theatre.

Murder by one brother nearly destroyed the life of the other. In shame and grief over his brother's actions, Edwin quit the stage, removed himself from public life, and never would have returned were it not for a bizarre twist of circumstances. Some months earlier, Edwin Booth had been present when a young man found himself pinned between a railcar and a crowded platform. That young man later wrote of this experience, saying:

In this situation the train began to move, and by the motion I was twisted off my feet, and had dropped somewhat, with feet downward, into the open space, and was personally helpless, when my coat collar was vigorously seized and I was quickly pulled up and out to a secure footing on the platform. Upon turning to thank my rescuer I saw it was Edwin Booth, whose face was of course well known to me, and I expressed my gratitude to him, and in doing so, called him by name.[1]

The boy Edwin saved was Abraham Lincoln's son, Robert.

Alcoholism and depression nearly destroyed the once-brilliant actor during the months following the assassination. According to Edwin's family and friends, only his memory of his earlier heroism saved him, and on January 3, 1866, he took the stage as Hamlet at Winter Garden Theatre in New York. A packed audience said by a thunderous standing ovation that, in their estimation, Edwin was nothing like his brother.

How can two boys with the same father, same mother, same upbringing, and even the same occupation, turn out so differently? The Booth brothers illustrate a principle that we will discover in our study of Scripture: All children possess both a bent toward good and a bent toward evil, and without parental involvement, the haphazard influence of the world may take them one way or the other. The parent's job is to know his or her child and, by active involvement, override the arbitrary influence of circumstances. To do that, parents must seek to discover what their child's bents are.

Knowledge of Internal Bents

"Train up a child in the way he should go" (Proverbs 22:6) might be paraphrased to read: "Adapt the training of your children to be in keeping with their individual gifts or bents—the God-given characteristics built into them at birth." Parents must be diligent and extremely sensitive to observe these bents in their children so they can cooperate with the right bents and correct the wrong bents in their children's character. Just what are these God-given characteristics? Let's first look at Psalm 139 to examine the good bents God has put in all of us; then we'll go to Psalms 51 and 58 to examine the bad.

Bent toward Good

God knows us long before our parents do. And His knowledge is not superficial; it searches to the depths of our being. He knows all our bents, even the most intricate. Notice how David describes God's intimate knowledge of his life.

O Lord, You have searched me and known me.
You know when I sit down and when I rise up;
You understand my thought from afar.
You scrutinize my path and my lying down,
And are intimately acquainted with all my ways. . . .
For You formed my inward parts;
You wove me in my mother's womb. (Psalm 139:1–3, 13)

The image in that last line conveys the idea of knitting something together. With that embryonic ball of yarn, God knits together each child. Each one is unique and bears God's own fingerprints. Continuing, David shows that God plans our lives, which He so diligently fashions in the cover of darkness.

> Your eyes have seen my
>   unformed substance;
> And in Your book were
>   all written,
> The days that were
>   ordained for me,
> When as yet there was
>   not one of them.
> (Psalm 139:16)

The phrase "Your eyes have seen my unformed substance" means something far more than God sitting in the grandstands and spectating while the child develops. The word *seen*, which means "watched over," is used in an active sense, like an architect who painstakingly watches over every detail of construction to make sure the builders adhere to the blueprints. The bents in a child's blueprint—at least the good ones—are designed by God, and He oversees their placement to the extent that even the very days of the child are laid out by God.

GETTING TO THE ROOT

Notice the words the psalmist used throughout Psalm 139 to speak of God's direct involvement in His creation: "You formed," "You wove," "I was made," "I was wrought." Then in verse 16, he wrote, "And in Your book were all written the days that were *ordained for me*" (emphasis added). Most English versions translate the Hebrew this way, but the literal meaning is more poetic. The Hebrew word used is *yasar*, which means "to form or fashion"—like what an artisan does when he or she molds clay, weaves tapestry, or carves wood. And we find the very same word used in Genesis 2:7 when God "formed man of dust from the ground."

Are you watching your children to discover their bents with the same diligence that God took in designing them? Are you studying the architecture of their physical and psychological make-up, looking for God's blueprint and appreciating each strategically placed detail in their personalities? Or have you ignored the existing structure and begun a building project of your own, with your own blueprints in mind?

Take some time to read Psalm 139:13–16. Answer the following questions.

Think about your child. What does Psalm 139:13–16 say about his or her value to God? How can you see God's design and purpose in his or her life? Be specific.

_____

_____

_____

_____

Read the passage carefully again, and write a single sentence using your child's name that summarizes the psalmist's thought. If you have more than one child, do this for each of them.

_____

_____

_____

_____

The sovereign Architect of heaven has given you a sacred and unique creation—that special child you have for only a limited time. Make the most of that time, won't you? Get started on the right foundation, and get to know the child God has so graciously entrusted to your care.

 ## Family Huddle

Set aside some time and take the better part of an evening to work through the following questions. Think about each of your children individually. Remember that the objective is not merely to fill in the blanks. If you write nothing but come away with a greater understanding of your child and a vision for his or her future, the goal has been met.

List the positive qualities you see in your children — the things that seem to be the strong points in their character or their abilities.

_____

_____

_____

_____

Suppose you were to walk into an inventor's workshop and see one of his projects on a table, nearly complete. If you had to guess what the invention did, you would naturally look at the attachments, see its power source, put all the clues together, and then make a guess. In the same way, look at your child's gifts, interests, temperament, and other qualities, and make a guess as to what God may have in mind for his or her future.

_____

_____

_____

_____

How can you give your child opportunities to explore this and other visions for his or her future?

_____

_____

_____

_____

What if your child fails? What if his or her interest fizzles? Focusing on both attitude and action, note below how you plan to react.

_____

_____

_____

_____

Now go before the Creator, and pray for your child. Some suggestions for your time with God are listed.

- Thank Him for the gift of your child.

- Ask Him to give you supernatural perception to discover your child's bents.

- Ask Him to inspire you as to how you can cooperate with those bents and help your child live up to his or her God-given potential.

- Dedicate yourself to giving your child back to God, and ask for His help in doing it.

Bent toward Evil

Fashioned in the image of God, your child bears the imprint of divinity. But he or she also bears the defacing effects of the Fall. Psalm 51:5 underscores this bent toward evil.

> Behold, I was brought forth in iniquity,
> And in sin my mother conceived me.

David was not saying that the act of conception is evil, but that at the time of birth he possessed a sinful nature. Psalm 58:1–5 touches on this idea:

> Do you judge uprightly, O sons of men?
> No, in heart you work unrighteousness;
> On earth you weigh out the violence of your hands.
> The wicked are estranged from the womb;
> These who speak lies go astray from birth.
> They have venom like the venom of a serpent;
> Like a deaf cobra that stops up its ear,
> So that it does not hear the voice of charmers,
> Or a skillful caster of spells.

Because every child comes with this bent toward evil that leaves no part of his or her being untouched, God expects parents to take an active role in His plan for their children. The only cure for a defective heart is to find a new one.

> For I was born a sinner—yes, from the moment my mother conceived me.
>
> —Psalm 51:5 NLT

Read Psalm 51:6–10 carefully. Consider these questions:

How much confidence does David seem to have in his own ability to overcome his bent toward evil?

_____

_____

_____

_____

Looking at Psalm 51:8, describe how the psalmist's awareness of his sin problem affected him. Have you seen this kind of sorrow in your child?

_____

_____

_____

_____

According to Psalm 51:10, how does the poet expect to solve his problem with sin?

_____

_____

_____

_____

In Psalm 51:5 the songwriter lamented the hopelessness of his sinful condition — a birth defect that gave him no hope of overcoming his selfish desires alone. In verse 10 he asked God for a new heart. The Hebrew culture thought of the heart as a person's whole inner being, consisting of their thoughts, feelings, and yearnings — the secret person that only they and God knew. So, to ask for a new heart is to ask for a complete transformation from the inside out. This same transformation occurs at the moment of salvation. Paul reflected on this complete renovation of a person:

> It wasn't so long ago that we ourselves were stupid and stubborn, dupes of sin, ordered every which way by our glands, going around with a chip on our shoulder, hated and hating back. But when God, our kind and loving Savior God, stepped

in, he saved us from all that. It was all his doing; we had nothing to do with it. He gave us a good bath, and we came out of it new people, washed inside and out by the Holy Spirit. Our Savior Jesus poured out new life so generously. (Titus 3:3–6 MSG)

The primary goal of a parent is to guide his or her child to salvation in Jesus Christ and allow Him to straighten the child's bent toward evil. The very best parenting skills will have limited effect unless the Holy Spirit gives the child a new, obedient heart.

A Point to Ponder

Just as physical characteristics are hereditary, so the personal characteristics of parents are passed down generation after generation. The following case in point is worthy of our attention:

> The father of Jonathan Edwards was a minister and his mother was the daughter of a clergyman. Among their descendants were fourteen presidents of colleges, more than one hundred college professors, more than one hundred lawyers, thirty judges, sixty physicians, more than a hundred clergymen, missionaries and theology professors, and about sixty authors. There is scarcely any great American industry that has not had one of his family among its chief promoters. Such is the product of one American Christian family, reared under the most favorable conditions.[2]

In Other Words

God sees us with the eyes of a Father. He sees our defects, errors, and blemishes. But He also sees our value.[3]

—Max Lucado

What qualities and character traits are you passing down to your children? Are you actively involved in knowing your children, guiding them toward maturity? Are you modeling God's love to them? Are you instilling in them a reverence and knowledge of Him as you seek to develop their positive bents? Or are you passively allowing their evil bents to run rampant? Remember, the legacy you leave will shape your family for generations to come.

6

A CHIP OFF THE OLD BENT
Exodus 34:5–8

Physicians tell us that deformities are often hereditary, as are certain diseases and predispositions to disease. Psychiatrists state that mental illnesses and emotional problems may also be inherited. It stands to reason, then, that certain spiritual characteristics may also be passed down from generation to generation.

Regarding spiritual genetics, our heritage contains three major aspects. First, every person is born in the image of God, with a God-given personality and distinct abilities (Genesis 1:26–27). Second, every person is born with a sin nature, a general bent toward evil inherited from Adam (Romans 5:12). Third, each of us has a specific bent or tendency toward evil inherited from our immediate forefathers. This third area will be our course of investigation in this chapter.

Evil Bent Defined and Explained

According to Scripture, everyone is born estranged from God (Psalms 51:5; 58:3; Romans 3:10–18; Ephesians 2:3; Colossians 1:21), and that separation stems from two main culprits.

Generally—from Adam

When Adam sinned in the Garden of Eden, he was acting as the representative of all humankind, and so his sin passed to each of us.

> Through one man sin entered into the world, and death
> through sin, and so death spread to all men, because all
> sinned. (Romans 5:12)

We can trace the root of our evil bent back to the first man. But the fruit of that bent—the evil thoughts, words, and actions themselves—can be traced more immediately to the branches of our own family tree.

Specifically—from Mom and Dad

Think about yourself for a minute. Chances are, if you take a good look in the mirror, you'll see a striking reflection of the weaknesses you saw in your parents. The resemblance may be a violent temper, deception, sexual weakness, or anxiety. If the characteristic was a dominant gene in your parents' spiritual chemistry, that trait has probably been passed down to you.

Talk to some people who know both you and your parents, and ask if they have noticed any inherited mannerisms or habits. Record some of their observations here.

_____

_____

_____

_____

Biblical Basis for Specific Bents toward Evil

By precept and example, the Bible demonstrates how specific bents toward evil branch out from each family tree. In Exodus 34:5–7, we discover that actual iniquity is transferred. Amid the clefts of Mount Sinai, Moses brushed with God's glory in an awesome daybreak encounter.

> The Lord descended in the cloud and stood there with him as he called upon the name of the Lord. Then the Lord passed by in front of him and proclaimed, "The Lord, the Lord God, compassionate and gracious, slow to anger, and abounding in lovingkindness and truth; who keeps

GETTING TO THE ROOT

Most people don't use the term *iniquity* in everyday life. Try slipping it into a conversation around the water cooler at work and see what kind of looks you get. *Iniquity* has such a religious connotation that we may forget it applies to everyone. The term comes from a Hebrew word meaning "to bend, to twist, to distort." Even when your intentions are good, your bent toward the bad will unconsciously distort many of your good deeds so that they come out "iniquity"–twisted.

lovingkindness for thousands, who forgives iniquity, transgression and sin; yet He will by no means leave the guilty unpunished, visiting the iniquity of fathers on the children and on the grandchildren to the third and fourth generations." (Exodus 34:5–7)

In Other Words

Can you think of any negative traits or habits in your life that have been in your family line for generations? Perhaps you can identify negative patterns such as alcoholism, verbal or physical abuse, pornography, racism, bitterness, or fear. These areas of bondage are anything you may have learned environmentally, anything to which you may be genetically predisposed, or any binding influence passed down through other means. Whatever the bondage may be, the Lord wants to rebuild, restore, and renew these areas of devastation.

We must face generational strongholds head-on. If we don't, they can remain almost unrecognizable—but they don't remain benign. Family strongholds continue to be the seedbed for all sorts of destruction. Oftentimes we've grown up with these chains and they feel completely natural. We consider them part of our personality rather than a strangling yoke.

Thankfully, Christians aren't doomed to live with our families' sins. The Cross of Calvary is enough to set us free from every yoke; God's Word is enough to make liberty a practical reality, no matter what those before us left as an "inheritance."

Before we parents die of fright, let's remember God is the only perfect parent. He's not cursing three or four generations over a little parental irritability. In fact, I don't believe he's calling a curse down on anyone. As believers under the New Covenant who have been cleansed by Christ's blood, I think the concept of generational sin applies to us through its powerful repercussions instead. I believe God is referring to a natural phenomenon described poignantly in Hosea 8:7, "They sow the wind and reap the whirlwind." Parents and grandparents must be very careful what they sow because it may reap the wind in their own lives and a whirlwind in the lives that follow.

Never underestimate, however, God's power to redirect and bless an entire family line for generations to come when we humble ourselves before him, confess our sins, and petition him for full redemption.[1]

—Beth Moore

One part of God's declaration to Moses may especially catch our attention: "Visiting the iniquity of fathers on the children and on the grandchildren to the third and fourth generations" (Exodus 34:7). At first glance this seems vengeful and unfair. Yet God could have allowed that same perversion to continue throughout the family's history, fraying the entire family line. But God says "No—it will have rippling effects only to the third and fourth generations." The scales, then, are weighted not on God's harshness but on His kindness, demonstrating that He is indeed compassionate, gracious, and abounding in lovingkindness.

A Case Study: Abraham's Family

Turning back the pages of Israel's history, we'll follow a specific bent—deception—through four generations.

Abraham

Abraham's propensity to shade the truth is brought to light in Genesis 12.

> Now there was a famine in the land; so Abram went down to Egypt to sojourn there, for the famine was severe in the land. It came about when he came near to Egypt, that he said to Sarai his wife, "See now, I know that you are a beautiful woman; and when the Egyptians see you, they will say, 'This is his wife'; and they will kill me, but they will let you live. Please say that you are my sister so that it may go well with me because of you, and that I may live on account of you."
> (Genesis 12:10–13)

The truth was that Sarah was Abraham's wife and half sister. But Abraham shaded that part of the truth. Looking further at Abraham's life, we see that this tendency to lie—a well-established bent in his character—crops up again and again (see also Genesis 20:1–5, 10–13).

Abraham reasoned that since Sarah was his father's daughter from another marriage, and therefore technically his half sister, he was speaking the truth. But he implied something entirely false—that she was *only* a sister.

Isaac

As Abraham's family tree spread its branches, the seeds of this trait cropped up in the second generation. The bent of lying sprouted in Isaac's life through a situation similar to the one his father had experienced years earlier.

So Isaac lived in Gerar. When the men of the place asked about his wife, he said, "She is my sister," for he was afraid to say, "my wife," thinking, "the men of the place might kill me on account of Rebekah, for she is beautiful." It came about, when he had been there a long time, that Abimelech king of the Philistines looked out through a window, and saw, and behold, Isaac was caressing his wife Rebekah. Then Abimelech called Isaac and said, "Behold, certainly she is your wife! How then did you say, 'She is my sister'?" And Isaac said to him, "Because I said, 'I might die on account of her.' " Abimelech said, "What is this you have done to us? One of the people might easily have lain with your wife, and you would have brought guilt upon us." (Genesis 26:6–10)

As we see this same crooked bent from Abraham resurfacing in Isaac's life, we can't help but think, "Like father, like son."

Jacob

Unchecked in Isaac's life, this flaw was passed from Isaac to his son Jacob. Isaac and Rebekah had twin sons, Jacob and Esau, with bents that went in different directions. At an early age Jacob began to develop a Machiavellian habit of doing whatever he needed to gain the advantage, no matter how manipulative (see Genesis 25:27–33).

Encouraged by his mother, Jacob allowed his habit to culminate in a treacherous act of deception. Jacob deceived his father, Isaac, into giving him the blessing that belonged to his brother.

Then Rebekah took the best garments of Esau her elder son, which were with her in the house, and put them on Jacob her younger son. And she put the skins of the young goats on his hands and on the smooth part of his neck. She also gave the savory food and the bread, which she had made, to her son Jacob.

Then he came to his father and said, "My father." And he said, "Here I am. Who are you, my son?" Jacob said to his father, "I am Esau your firstborn; I have done as you told me. Get up, please, sit and eat of my game, that you may bless me." Isaac said to his son, "How is it that you have it so quickly, my son?" And he said, "Because the Lord your God caused it to happen to me." Then Isaac said to Jacob, "Please come close,

that I may feel you, my son, whether you are really my son
Esau or not." So Jacob came close to Isaac his father, and he felt
him and said, "The voice is the voice of Jacob, but the hands
are the hands of Esau." He did not recognize him, because his
hands were hairy like his brother Esau's hands; so he blessed
him. And he said, "Are you really my son Esau?" And he said,
"I am." So he said, "Bring it to me, and I will eat of my son's
game, that I may bless you." And he brought it to him, and he
ate; he also brought him wine and he drank. Then his father
Isaac said to him, "Please come close and kiss me, my son." So
he came close and kissed him; and when he smelled the smell
of his garments, he blessed him. (Genesis 27:15–27)

So entrenched was this habit of lying that even when Jacob was old,
deception continued to persist in his life (see Genesis 43:2–6).

The Sons of Jacob

Tragically, Jacob's habit of deception became so ingrained that it left an
imprint in the lives of his sons.

Like his parents, Jacob had his family favorites, the foremost being Joseph.
But the other sons resented this. And, in a jealous rage over the interpretation of a dream Joseph had, the other brothers sold him to a slave caravan. To
cover the crime, they took Joseph's distinctive, multicolored coat, dipped it
in animal's blood, and brought it to their father, explaining, "We found this;
please examine it to see whether it is your son's tunic or not" (Genesis 37:32).
The whole scene, props and all, was staged. The second lie was unspoken:

Then [Jacob] examined it and said, "It is my son's tunic. A wild
beast has devoured him; Joseph has surely been torn to pieces!"
(37:33)

Jacob went into mourning, and his sons did not say a word. By their
silence, they lied. Like father, like sons.

Some Suggestions to Sincere yet Struggling Parents

A lesson like this can be depressing, particularly when we see the skel-
etons of our own character flaws being fleshed out in our children. How can
we keep from passing on those destructive bents? Consider the following four
suggestions.

First: Lead your child to faith in Christ. The first and biggest step in straightening out the bents is for your child to become aligned with Jesus, who is "the way, and the truth, and the life" (John 14:6). The Holy Spirit makes that alignment possible because He works internally to create a pliable spirit.

Second: Ask for God's wisdom in studying your child. Observe your child's words (Luke 6:45) and actions (1 Timothy 5:25), because they reflect character . . . or the lack of it.

Third: As you set limits, be fair and consistent. Consistency is what shapes character over the long haul. It gives your children the security they need to entrust themselves into your hands.

Fourth: Do everything in your power to maintain open and loving communication with your child. You will never know your child intimately unless you take control of your schedule and plan time just to listen and observe. This may require putting the TV to bed early instead of the children. Or how about taking your child to work one day instead of bringing your work home? Whatever it takes, your child is worth it!

Family Huddle

Take a moment now to examine how effectively you're applying these suggestions for preventing bad bents in your children.

	Doing Great	Making Progress	Need Help!
Leading your child to faith in Christ	❏	❏	❏
Asking for God's wisdom in studying your child	❏	❏	❏
As you're setting limits, being fair and consistent	❏	❏	❏
Doing everything in your power to maintain open and loving communication with your child	❏	❏	❏

How are you doing at preventing bad bents from forming? Do you sometimes find yourself in need of help? If so, take the time to plan a strategy for improving one of these weaker areas.

The area I'll begin working on is:

_____

The strategy I'll begin implementing is:

_____

_____

_____

_____

_____

7

Shaping the Will with Wisdom
Selected Proverbs

While growing up, many of us came to associate the word *discipline* with only one thing: punishment—usually of the dreaded "wait till your father gets home" variety.

But as Bruce Ray explains in his book *Withhold Not Correction*, discipline is more than simply punishment.

> Biblical discipline is *correction*, and that means that the pattern of the child's behavior must be *changed by instruction* in righteousness. He must be shown the error of his way, and then directed to the proper path. This requires explanation and instruction. Biblical discipline demands words.[1]

Too many parents rely on punishment alone to discipline their children. By doing that, they're neglecting to give their kids the assistance they need in understanding and applying God's Word to their lives.

How well prepared are you to shape your children's wills with the wisdom of God's Word? Are you training them in the way they should go or punishing them for going in the way they shouldn't? The objective in child rearing is not for parents to win the tug-of-war at all costs. If you do, you may end up not only with a muddy, tearful child, but also with a relationship strained beyond repair. Rather, your objective is to shape the will, gently yet firmly, as a potter would a clay vase. But that takes a special kind of wisdom—a wisdom only God can provide.

Model Your Heavenly Father

Proverbs, a storehouse of godly wisdom, tells us that if we truly love our children, we'll discipline them. Turn to Proverbs 13:24 and read it carefully.

This verse contrasts two kinds of parents: one who neglects to act when the child does wrong and another who addresses his child's misconduct with a swift and appropriate response. Notice the way the one who loves his child disciplines him—"diligently."

When you think of diligent people you know, which of the following words would you use to describe them?

_____ Angry	_____ Patient	_____ Consistent
_____ Level-headed	_____ Harsh	_____ Reasoned
_____ Hot-tempered	_____ Self-centered	_____ Others-centered

Recall the last time the Lord turned your attitude from a desire to sin to a desire to please Him. Did His methods of producing change in your heart harm you or help you? What did His discipline teach you about His character?

_____

_____

_____

_____

In Other Words

It is obvious that children are aware of the contest of wills between generations, and that is precisely why the parental response is so important. When a child behaves in ways that are disrespectful or harmful to himself or others, his hidden purpose is often to verify the stability of the boundaries. This testing has much the same function as a policeman who turns doorknobs at places of business after dark. Though he tries to open doors, he hopes they are locked and secure. Likewise, a child who assaults the loving authority of his parents is greatly reassured when their leadership holds firm and confident. He finds his greatest security in a structured environment where the rights of other people (and his own) are protected by definite boundaries.[2]

— Dr. James Dobson

God makes it clear in His Word that an unresponsive, lax parent does more harm than good to his or her children. Kids actually crave the security of consistent boundaries. If we desire to demonstrate God's love to our children, we'll model His compassion, kindness, and patience as well as His fairness, justice, and persistence as we set firm boundaries for our kids.

Some Necessary Distinctions Worth Making

Hebrews 12:6 tells us that the Lord disciplines those He loves. Just as the Lord intervenes in our lives when we stray too far from Him, we need to intervene when our children make defiant choices. We want to shape their character, but not crush their spirit. With all the parenting advice out there, it can be hard to decipher how to do that God's way. To get started, let's make some clear distinctions on some potentially problematic topics.

Abuse versus Discipline

Because child abuse has reached tragic proportions, many people avoid any kind of discipline. But a difference exists between the two: abuse tears down a child's spirit; discipline builds it up.

Abuse is unfair, extreme, and degrading. Abusive actions are unduly harsh, unnecessarily long, and totally inappropriate. If we drag our children's feelings through the mud and kick them when they're down, then we're being abusive. The result? Soiled self-esteem and scars that often last a lifetime. Actions like that are not discipline; they're abuse. And abuse doesn't grow out of love; it stems from hate.

Discipline is fair, fitting, and upholds the child's dignity. Discipline is built on a foundation of justice. Loving discipline isn't capricious or arbitrary, so the child should have a good idea of the punishment that will be meted out if parental boundaries are willfully and defiantly violated. This form of correction strengthens rather than shatters the child's self-worth. Discipline is rooted in proper motivation—love and genuine concern—not in anger or expedience.

Crushing versus Shaping

Proverbs 15:13 paints a vivid contrast between a spirit that has been shaped and one that has been crushed.

> A joyful heart makes a cheerful face,
> But when the heart is sad, the spirit is broken.

Proverbs 17:22 says similarly:

> A joyful heart is good medicine,
> But a broken spirit dries up the bones.

The ultimate goal of discipline is to build up children with direction and confidence, giving them a strong and secure self-esteem to carry them through life. Shaping the will nurtures vitality for living, while crushing the will "dries up" that vitality.

Look back on the last time you disciplined each of your children. On the following chart, write down each of your children's names and his or her wrongdoing, how you felt when it occurred, how you reacted to it in the moment, the discipline you chose, and the goal of that discipline.

Child's Name	Child's Wrongdoings	Your Feelings	Your Reaction	Chosen Discipline	Goal of Chosen Discipline

Did your discipline flow from your emotions (anger, embarrassment, fear), or from a desire to shape your child's character?

_____

_____

_____

_____

Did your chosen discipline shape your child, or did it shame your child? How do you know?

_____

_____

_____

_____

When our children mess up, we find it easy to lash out at them with hot-headed words and hasty actions and call it discipline. Exercising true discipline—calming our emotions, considering whether or not the offense was willfully defiant, and responding with firm but fair consequences—is much more difficult.

Natural Childishness versus Willful Defiance

In their early years, every child needs space in which to learn, make mistakes, and develop. As a parent, you must learn to distinguish between childish irresponsibility and willfully disobedient behavior.

> A child should not be spanked for behavior that is not willfully defiant. When he forgets to feed the dog or make his bed or take out the trash—when he leaves your tennis racket outside in the rain or loses his bicycle—remember that these behaviors are typical of childhood. It is, more than likely, the mechanism by which an immature mind is protected from adult anxieties and pressures. Be gentle as you teach him to do better. If he fails to respond to your patient instruction, it then becomes appropriate to administer some well-defined consequences (he may have to work to pay for the item he abused or be deprived of its use, etc.). However, childish irresponsibility is very different from willful defiance, and should be handled more patiently.[3]

Place an **I** for irresponsibility or a **D** for defiance in the blank next to the following actions:

_____ Leaving the milk out on the kitchen counter and letting it spoil

_____ Repeatedly demanding food for dinner other than what is being served

_____ Getting a detention for forgetting to bring a book to class

_____ Getting a detention for smarting off to the teacher

Several Suggestions Worth Considering

Shaping the will with wisdom is a critical task of parenting. The following suggestions should make it easier and more effective.

Start Early

Let's look again at the word *diligently* in Proverbs 13:24 to find wisdom for carrying out this awesome responsibility.

> He who spares his rod hates his son,
> But he who loves him disciplines him diligently.

The association of *diligence* with *discipline* indicates that we should start disciplining our children early in their lives. The longer we wait to begin the process, the more difficult it will become. Consider the words of Proverbs 19:18:

> Discipline your son while
>   there is hope
> And do not desire
>   his death.

The man who spares the rod *hates* his child (Proverbs 13:24). The one who fails to discipline his child *desires his death* (19:18). These strong words show us that the father or mother who withholds discipline actually harms his or her child. Don't mistake lax standards for love. Our children need us to correct them so that they will know right from wrong—so that they will leave our homes and build their own strong families.

GETTING TO THE ROOT

The word *diligently* has a colorful background in Hebrew. Originally, the Hebrew word meant "dawn" or "early morning." Later it evolved into the idea of pursuing something early in life—like a career—and thus came to mean "with determination" or "with steadfastness."

Stay Balanced

Balance is what keeps children from falling off their bicycles and skinning their knees. Balance is also what keeps parents from crashing when it comes to disciplining their children. Two kinds of discipline are mentioned in the Bible. Both complement each other, but both must be kept in balance.

First, let's look at *physical discipline*. Proverbs 22:15 describes this category of discipline.

> Foolishness is bound up in the heart of a child;
> The rod of discipline will remove it far from him.

The rod indicates the infliction of pain. Dr. James Dobson underscores the importance of the child being able to associate wrongdoing with pain.

> If your child has ever bumped his arm against a hot stove,
> you can bet he'll never deliberately do that again. He does not

become a more violent person because the stove burned him; in fact, he learned a valuable lesson from the pain. Similarly, when he falls out of his high chair or smashes his finger in the door or is bitten by a grumpy dog, he learns about physical dangers in the world. These bumps and bruises throughout childhood are nature's way of teaching what to fear. They do not damage self-esteem. They do not make vicious people. They acquaint the individual with reality. In like manner, an appropriate spanking from a loving parent provides the same service. It says there are not only physical dangers to be avoided, but one must steer clear of such social traps as selfishness, defiance, dishonesty, and unprovoked aggression.[4]

The second kind of discipline is *verbal discipline*. This category of correction, also known as "reproof," is found in Proverbs 3:11–12.

> My son, do not reject the discipline of the Lord
> Or loathe His reproof,
> For whom the Lord loves He reproves,
> Even as a father corrects the son in whom he delights.

"Reproof" does not indicate a tongue-lashing with cutting remarks that lacerate character. Instead, reproof is verbal instruction arising out of a genuine and deep-felt delight in the child (note the word *delights* in verse 12). Proverbs 29:15 shows verbal reproof in balance with physical discipline: "The rod and reproof give wisdom."

Be Consistent

When you're under pressure, you may find it easy to let convenience determine how and when you discipline your child—a case of the urgent squeezing out the important. But the rule shouldn't be expediency; it should be consistency. These guidelines will help to ensure that your discipline will be consistent:

1. Make sure the rules are known beforehand.

2. Discipline privately.

3. Explain the violation and its consequences.

4. Administer the rod soundly.

5. Tenderly hold your child after the spanking.

6. Assure your child of your love and concern.

Be Reasonable

As a child grows older, there comes a time when spanking him or her is inappropriate. If you're not sensitive to this, you will end up demeaning rather than disciplining your child. Older kids still need discipline, though, so an effective parent will implement age-appropriate punishments.

In a world full of physical and verbal abuse, knowing when to spank, when to ground, and when to use firm words can be challenging. Before you act, ask yourself, "How is this spanking, grounding, or reproof going to help my child?" "Am I doing this out of emotion or out of a desire for my child's good?" "Do I need to take a breather before I breathe another word?" "Is this punishment an appropriate and fair consequence for my child's actions?"

Consider the Source

A fascinating link often exists between how you were disciplined as a child and how you discipline your children. Review the four "suggestions worth considering" in this section and then reflect on how your parents disciplined you.

Were they diligent about starting early? When did they start?

_____

_____

Did they balance the physical and verbal aspects of your discipline? How?

_____

_____

Was the discipline consistent in your home? Explain.

_____

_____

How reasonable do you think your parents were? Why?

_____

_____

If you have children at home, write out how you can use the suggestions from this study to wisely discipline them. Note especially the areas you feel need to be changed from the way you were brought up.

_____

_____

_____

Significant Goals Worth Implementing

You may miss the mark on discipline from time to time, but if you don't have a goal in sight, you're likely to miss every time you try. To stay on target, consider aiming for these goals as you seek to shape your child's will with wisdom.

For Yourself

Model God's role of authority until your child reaches the point of a natural transfer of that authority from you to God.

At what point do you think we start letting go of our children and letting God lead them directly rather than through us? Explain.

_____

_____

_____

Why do we find it difficult to let go of our kids even when they're old enough to be under God's authority alone?

_____

_____

_____

For Your Children

Help them cultivate a healthy respect for themselves and others so they can be strong enough and secure enough to stand up under the pressures of life. Let's remember that our job as parents is to work ourselves out of a job. Our kids need to leave the nest by flying rather than by falling to the ground with undeveloped or broken wings. While a lack of discipline can leave them unable to fly, harsh punishment can leave them permanently injured.

Family Huddle

Take some time to check the effectiveness of your discipline by checking your kids' and your own perspectives. Ask the following questions over dinner or in the car when you have time to talk.

- What movie or television character reminds you most of my (our) parenting style?

- If one of your friends asked you how I (we) was unfair or unreasonable with you, what would you say?

- When you do something wrong, how do you feel when I (we) punish you?

- Do you think my (our) punishments fit your wrongdoing? If not, how would you adjust them if you could?

- What words have I (we) said in the last week that have made you angry, hurt, or sad?

- What words have I (we) said in the last week that have made you smile?

If your kids are younger and can't answer these questions, or if they're teens who don't talk much, observe their faces and their body language in the heat of your next disagreement. Their expressions and their gestures reveal their feelings.

8

ENHANCING ESTEEM
Selected Proverbs

One of the greatest contributions family members can make to one another is to enhance each person's self-esteem, their sense of personal value and worth. Odds are, if it doesn't happen at home, it probably won't happen at all. Unfortunately, family members are often better at putting each other down than building each other up. They use their words as swords rather than salve, to hurt rather than to heal.

> There is one who speaks rashly like the thrusts of a sword,
> But the tongue of the wise brings healing. (Proverbs 12:18)

Contrary to the childhood chant, "Sticks and stones may break my bones, but words will never hurt me," cutting words do hurt. They penetrate deeply into a person's heart, slashing self-esteem to ribbons. In this chapter, we'll take a closer look at what self-esteem is and then examine some ways to enhance self-esteem in our loved ones rather than erode it.

The Essential Value of Self-Esteem

In Ephesians 5, we find two biblical reasons for cultivating self-esteem, both in ourselves and in others. Paul wrote about the marriage relationship in this passage, but the principles he explained have a much broader application as well.

> Husbands, love your wives, just as Christ also loved the church
> and gave Himself up for her, so that He might sanctify her,
> having cleansed her by the washing of water with the word,
> that He might present to Himself the church in all her glory,
> having no spot or wrinkle or any such thing; but that she
> would be holy and blameless. So husbands ought also to love

their own wives as their own bodies. For no one ever hated his own flesh, but nourishes and cherishes it, just as Christ also does the church, because we are members of His body. (Ephesians 5:25–30)

Reason One: A good self-esteem is God's desire for us because it provides the foundation to love others. Paul helps us answer the question, "Why should we love ourselves?" Loving ourselves enables us to unselfishly love others. It also allows us to bring out the best in others, as Christ does with us. The love we show our spouses, or anyone else, is in direct proportion to the love we have for ourselves. And this love for ourselves is not a noisy conceit, but a quiet sense of self-worth.

If you loved others the way you love yourself, what would your actions look like? What motives would be behind these actions?

_____

_____

_____

Reason Two: We should have a healthy self-esteem because God sees worth and value in each of us. We are nourished and cherished by Christ Himself. We can esteem ourselves and can help others esteem themselves because the Creator and Savior of all cherishes us.

Vital Elements of Self-Esteem

In *The Sensation of Being Somebody*, author Maurice Wagner writes that the three essentials of healthy self-esteem are *belongingness*, feeling accepted and wanted by others; *worthiness*, having a sense of value; and *competence*, feeling adequate to carry out life's daily situations. "These three feelings," Wagner explains, "blend together in the formation of self-concept like three tones of a musical chord. At times each can be considered separately, but usually it is impossible to distinguish one from the other."[1]

The harmonious tones of a healthy self-esteem can be disrupted, however, by the discordant notes of hostility, guilt, and fear.

Hostility contradicts feelings of belongingness; guilt cancels feelings of worthiness. Hostility says, in effect, "You are bad, I don't like you." Guilt says, "I am bad, you could not like me. I loathe myself.". . .

Fear tends to paralyze the mind and cause it to function inadequately. Fear and its close associate, anxiety, cancel the "I can" feelings of competence so that a person is inclined to think "I can't" about many things.[2]

Just as a sensitive conductor can detect a flat note while listening to a full orchestra, so too, sensitive parents can detect a flat note of self-esteem in their family by listening to the prevailing tone of the family.

Play back in your mind the family conversations you've participated in or heard over the last couple of days. Now do this again, only this time erase the actual words and simply listen to the family tone and what's being communicated by it. Do the conversations in your home resonate with belongingness, worthiness, and competence? Or is there a cacophony of hostility, guilt, and fear?

Is there a flat note in the self-esteem of one of your children? Which of the three tones—belongingness, worthiness, or competence—needs tuning? How can you tune it?

_____

_____

_____

_____

Sources of Self-Esteem

Today a variety of equations for building your child's self-esteem are offered by society. As Wagner notes, the trouble is that none of them balance.

> One such equation is *Appearance + Admiration = a Whole Person.* This equation does not balance because we are not the sum and total of how we appear or what others admiringly think of us.

> Another such equation which does not balance is *Performance + Accomplishments = a Whole Person.* We are more than the sum total of our skills and the recognized abilities we have developed.

> A third equation might be *Status + Recognition = a Whole Person.* This equation is also untrue, for we are more than anyone thinks of us.[3]

None of these equations provide lasting satisfaction of our need for belongingness, worthiness, and competence. Appearance, performance, and status are all pawns of circumstance. None of them come with any guarantees.

Wagner concludes that the only equation that truly balances is *God + Me = a Whole Person*. And this is guaranteed.

> The meaning of the equation of self-identity, *God + Me = a Whole Person*, is this: My belongingness is secured and reaffirmed by my love for God my Father and validated by His love for me. My worthiness is secured and reaffirmed by my love for Jesus Christ His Son and validated by His love for me. My competence is secured and reaffirmed in daily situations of life through the ministry and love of the Holy Spirit as He uses the Word of God to instruct, correct, and reassure me; my competence is validated as I live by the Word of God.[4]

Looking back, can you identify which equation you were raised to believe?

_____

_____

_____

_____

Which are you teaching your children today? (Hint: Consider which equation is reflected most in your lifestyle and attitudes.)

_____

_____

_____

_____

Components of Esteem's Development

GETTING TO THE ROOT

The Greek word for *nourish* is *ektrepho*. Its root, *trepho*, can mean "to bring," and the prefix *ek* means "out." *Ektrepho* is most often used in a context relating to children, as in Ephesians 6:4, and has the idea of feeding, caring for, and drawing out the child. The word implies that some things are deep within the child and need to be drawn out by the parents.

The Greek word for *cherish* is *thalpo*, meaning "to heat or keep warm." In the Greek translation of the Hebrew Old Testament, this word is used of a bird sitting on her eggs (Deuteronomy 22:6). In the New Testament this same word is used of the tenderness of a nursing mother (1 Thessalonians 2:7).

From Paul's marital insights in Ephesians 5:28–30, two important actions can be taken to enhance the development of self-esteem in our children. Paul wrote:

> He who loves his own wife loves himself; for no one ever hated his own flesh, but nourishes and cherishes it, just as Christ also does the church, because we are members of His body.

The first component of the love we show others is found in the word *nourish*. The second component is revealed in the word *cherish*. Putting together the two components of nourishing and cherishing conveys the distinct impression that enhancing your child's self-esteem requires a great amount of attention and affection. Within every child are certain God-given characteristics. As those characteristics are "drawn out" and "warmed," the self-esteem of that child begins to grow stronger.

What characteristics do you see in your loved ones that you could draw out and warm so that their self-esteem would grow stronger? If you don't have children, think of the people in your life whom you do influence.

Name	Characteristics	Ways to draw out or affirm characteristics

Compensations for Esteem's Absence

When self-esteem is lacking, people often put up defenses—covering up, rationalizing, or aggressively asserting themselves. They may also wear masks—plastic smiles or constant frowns—to hide their hurt or insecurity. You may have heard the saying: Scratch a humorist and you'll find a sad man. Humor often becomes a mask for a hurting person to hide behind—ask any comedian. Onstage humor often stems from offstage hurt, a truth Proverbs 14:13 corroborates—"Even in laughter the heart may be in pain."

Culmination of Esteem's Presence

When your children have strong self-esteem, they are free to be everything God created them to be. They can accept and love others because they have first accepted and loved themselves. And they will have a calm sense of security and a deep sense of satisfaction independent of performance or peer recognition.

Are you committed to giving your children the invaluable gift of a strong sense of self-worth? If so, it will be reflected in your words. Words like, "Nice try, Son" or "Thanks, Honey. That was so thoughtful of you."

Are those the kind of words that greet your children when they come home from school? Or do the words "How many times have I told you . . ." or "Do it right or don't do it at all" cut into their tender hearts?

Remember, life and death are in the power of the tongue. You can bring about the life of your child's self-esteem, or its death.

Family Huddle

Are you ready for a reality check on your words? Keep three jars in your kitchen—one with sour candy, one with sweet candy, and one with blank slips of paper in it. Put the same number of candies in the sour jar and in the sweet jar. Then tell your children that they can have a piece of candy from the sour jar every time your words hurt them and a piece from the sweet jar every time your words encourage them. In return for the candy, they must write their name, the words they heard, and how those words made them feel on a piece of paper from the third jar. As you watch the levels of candy drop, you'll see how your words are affecting your kids. Don't ask them to explain their choice of candy in the moment. Instead, at the end of the week, open the third jar together as a family and discuss the notes from your kids to you. You'll all learn a lot!

Cornerstone of Esteem's Development

How can a parent know what they should build up in their children? Use God's wisdom. From the wealth of Proverbs come three gems of wisdom—parental qualities your children will treasure forever.

First: A commitment to discover. Deep within the heart are concealed the secrets of one's life, hidden away like a subterranean spring. Parents, therefore, must be committed to digging down deep and drawing out that sparkling water hidden in their children.

> A plan in the heart of a man is like deep water,
> But a man of understanding draws it out. (Proverbs 20:5)

How willing are you to invest time in your children in order to discover how they see themselves? For one week, keep a journal of the time you spend really talking to your kids, and summarize what you learn below.

_____

_____

_____

_____

Second: A willingness to get involved. As a file hones the edges of a knife, so a sharpening of the soul occurs when two people intimately and intensely interact.

> Iron sharpens iron,
> So one man sharpens another. (Proverbs 27:17)

If your family wants to sharpen each other emotionally, you have to get involved emotionally. If you want to sharpen each other spiritually, you must get involved spiritually. If you want to sharpen each other mentally, you need to get involved mentally. You need to be there for your children, actively helping them grow.

What is one significant way you get more involved with your kids or the people in your life?

_____

_____

_____

_____

Third: An ability to reflect. Just as we need mirrors around the house to see if our hair is in place, so we need family members to reflect our inner self to us—to show us what's going on inside. In that reflection our identity comes into focus.

> As in water face reflects face,
> So the heart of man reflects man. (Proverbs 27:19)

Children also see just how much they are valued in our eyes. And, as water reflects best when calm and still, so do we.

What's the difference between time spent together and quality time invested in each other? Which is more prevalent in your relationships?

_____

_____

_____

_____

Do you want to enhance your children's self-esteem? Then commit to helping them *discover* the spiritual equation for a healthy self-esteem. Get *involved* in teaching them the eternal biblical truths the equation rests upon. And finally, *reflect* these truths in your relationships with your children.

Personal Ways to Encourage Self-Esteem

By now, you may be asking, "How do I, as a parent, discover my child? How do I get involved? How do I reflect?" Try these two ways to begin to do those things and thus enhance your child's self-worth.

Develop good, open communication. Good communication is not made up of churchy little homilies complete with organ accompaniment, but consists of real talk for the real world. Pious words from the pulpit won't cut it—your children need transparent teaching from your own life.

Help each child compensate. Find areas of strength in your children's lives, and help them develop these to compensate for weaker areas. If a child isn't athletic, for example, focus on artistic or musical development. Help your children discover their unique, God-given abilities and talents.

A Concluding Thought

In his poem "I Love You," Roy Croft shows how love cherishes and nourishes . . . how it discovers, gets involved, and reflects . . . how it draws out and develops the loved one's self-esteem.

I love you,
Not only for what you are
But for what I am
When I am with you.

I love you,
Not only for what
You have made of yourself,
But for what
You are making of me.

I love you,
For the part of me
That you bring out;
I love you
For putting your hand
Into my heaped-up heart
And passing over
All the foolish, weak things
That you can't help
Dimly seeing there,
And for drawing out
Into the light
All the beautiful belongings
That no one else had looked
Quite far enough to find.

I love you because you
Are helping me to make
Of the lumber of my life
Not a tavern
But a temple;
Out of works
Of my every day
Not a reproach
But a song.[5]

9

CHALLENGING YEARS OF ADOLESCENCE (PART ONE)
Selected Scriptures

Adolescence. Webster defines the term as "the state or process of growing up."[1] Sounds simple enough, right? But we all know that adolescence represents one of the toughest times of a person's life.

Remember when hormones raced through your body like horses out of a starting gate? No doubt, you grew interested in getting to know those of the opposite sex, but you were a little scared, too. Men, maybe your voice cracked to broadcast that you weren't a man yet. Ladies, perhaps a huge pimple erupted on your nose on the night before your "big date." *Remember?*

Adolescence closed the door on childhood. We set aside our G.I. Joe action figures and Barbie dolls to focus on girlfriends and boyfriends. We forgot all about our model cars when Dad let us borrow the keys to *his* car. Dress-up clothes gave way to prom dresses and graduation robes. Lazy vacation days faded into memories as summer jobs and other responsibilities took precedence.

Once we reached adolescence, childhood was behind us, forever locked away. There we stood on the threshold of adult life with great anticipation and fear. We felt all eyes on us as we prepared to take that uncertain step into the world of the grown-ups. We wanted to take our time and enter that world gracefully. But the confusion, anxiety, and excitement built until finally we stumbled unceremoniously into adulthood.

Four Questions Adolescents Ask

During this time of struggling and soul searching, adolescents, understandably, begin to replace exclamation points with question marks. As they grope to find their balance and stand on their own two feet, at times they question their foundation, their faith, and their values. The questions young people ask generally fall into four main categories.

Who Am I?

The first question emerges from adolescents' struggle to find their *identity*. As everything begins to change in a teenager's life, the question, "Who is the real me?" becomes central.

Which Attitudes Will I Choose?

Prior to adolescence, a child learns to listen to and submit to Mom and Dad. But, as that child begins to grow up, questions of *responsibility* arise. In childhood, the consequences of irresponsible behavior were buffered by parents. Adulthood, however, has a way of exacting consequences for irresponsible decisions. Adolescents want increasing independence from their parents, but they often struggle to accept the responsibilities that accompany independence.

Whose Role Will I Respect?

This question involves the struggle over *authority*. As adolescents try to discover where they fit into society, they also begin to question the pillars of authority that undergird that society. Authority figures can be found everywhere: parents, teachers, principals, coaches, employers, pastors, political leaders, media figures, and role models. "Whom should I follow? How far? And for how long?" Questions like these flood the minds of today's teenagers.

What Will Be My Lifestyle?

Before adolescence, most children adopt their parents' values. If their parents avoid alcohol, they do, too. If their parents go to church, the kids go along. If their parents value education, so do they. But when adolescence emerges, all of those previously held values are suddenly up for grabs. Adolescents struggle with *conformity*. Teens ask themselves, "What do *I* want to do? Which road will my life take? The way of my parents? My peers? The public? Will I be a follower and adopt someone else's lifestyle, or will I chart a path of my own?"

The Struggles of Two Biblical Adolescents

To demonstrate that the struggles of adolescents aren't confined to those in our generation, let's examine the lives of two biblical adolescents—Jephthah and Absalom. As we take a look at some incidents from their adolescent days, we'll see how their responses helped shape their adult life with regard to *identity* and *responsibility.*

Jephthah's Struggle with Identity

Judges 11 introduces us to Jephthah:

> Now Jephthah the Gileadite was a valiant warrior, but he was the son of a harlot. And Gilead was the father of Jephthah. Gilead's wife bore him sons; and when his wife's sons grew up, they drove Jephthah out and said to him, "You shall not have an inheritance in our father's house, for you are the son of another woman." So Jephthah fled from his brothers and lived in the land of Tob; and worthless fellows gathered themselves about Jephthah, and they went out with him. (Judges 11:1–3)

Unwanted and rejected, Jephthah struggled with his identity. Cut out of his father's will and kicked out of his own home, Jephthah asked himself, "Who am I?" For an answer, he turned to his friends—a gang of good-for-nothings, the type of people that the book of Proverbs warns us about. As he hung out with these unsavory characters, Jephthah desperately tried to "find himself."

Before we go further into Jephthah's story, let's consider an important issue revealed in his life—the influence of his friends. The book of Proverbs reminds us of the value of good friends and the harm done by bad ones:

> He who walks with wise
> men will be wise,

GETTING TO THE ROOT

Scripture calls Jephthah "a valiant warrior." In Hebrew, the term for *valiant, chayil,* means "strong, capable, excellent, efficient, and powerful."[2] In contrast, the term used to describe Jephthah's friends is *req,* translated "worthless" and meaning "empty, vain, foolish, and idle."[3]

But the companion of fools will suffer harm. (Proverbs 13:20)

Jephthah fell into the companionship of fools—"worthless fellows," Scripture calls them. If you're a parent, do you know who your kids' friends are? Have you ever talked with your kids about the qualities of a good friend? Are you equipping your teens to make good decisions regarding their choice of friends? If you want to help them grow wisely into adulthood, you should be helping them to choose good friends. The shape of your children's future will be molded in large part by those who surround them, and those people most likely will be their peers rather than their parents or other authority figures.

Take a moment now to read Judges 11:4–11. You'll see that even as an adult, Jephthah searched for identity and longed for acceptance. That's what made the offer to be leader over all who lived in Gilead so appealing to him, despite his deep feelings of resentment over being rejected by his brothers. Jephthah's valor as a great warrior enabled him to become head and chief over the people of Gilead. As a result, he finally received the respect and acceptance that he had sought all his life.

Absalom's Struggle with Responsibility

Now let's examine the life of King David's son Absalom. Absalom struggled with fierce anger because his sister, Tamar, had been raped by her half brother Amnon. Not only that, but King David had responded passively to the news of this outrage and had refused to hold Amnon responsible for his crime. As a result, Absalom was left to fit together a jigsaw puzzle of conflicting loyalties and emotions. He puzzled over his responsibility toward his sister and toward Amnon, wondering, "Which attitudes and actions should I choose?"

For two years after this incident, resentment toward his father David stirred in Absalom's heart. And his hatred toward Amnon simmered until it came to a boil. Finally, the seething cauldron of this young man's resentment and hatred spilled over into an act of vengeance as he commanded his servants to kill Amnon.

After Amnon's murder was carried out, Absalom fled and went to stay with Talmai, the king of Geshur. The Bible tells us that not only did David mourn for Amnon, he also mourned for his son Absalom every day (see 2 Samuel 13:37).

To whom did Absalom run? Talmai was his maternal grandfather (see 2 Samuel 3:3). And what was he looking for? A lot of things: roots, security, acceptance, direction. For three years, Absalom stayed with Talmai. Then, after some persuasion from Joab, David had Absalom brought back to Jerusalem, but something was wrong.

> However [David] the king said, "Let him turn to his own
> house, and let him not see my face." So Absalom turned to his
> own house and did not see the king's face. (2 Samuel 14:24)

After a three-year absence, you would think Absalom and David would have wanted to see each other, talk things out, and make things right. But they had erected a wall of resentment between them. For two years, Absalom lived in Jerusalem, and for two years that wall separated father and son. As Absalom grew from adolescence into adulthood, he attempted to hurdle the wall in an effort to see his father and to remove the bitter stones that stood between them.

> Then Absalom sent for Joab, to send him to the king, but he would
> not come to him. So he sent again a second time, but he would not
> come. Therefore he said to his servants, "See, Joab's field is next to
> mine, and he has barley there; go and set it on fire." So Absalom's
> servants set the field on fire. Then Joab arose, came to Absalom at
> his house and said to him, "Why have your servants set my field
> on fire?" Absalom answered Joab, "Behold, I sent for you, saying,
> 'Come here, that I may send you to the king, to say, "Why have
> I come from Geshur? It would be better for me still to be there."'
> Now therefore, let me see the king's face, and if there is iniquity in
> me, let him put me to death." So when Joab came to the king and
> told him, he called for Absalom. Thus he came to the king and
> prostrated himself on his face to the ground before the king, and
> the king kissed Absalom. (2 Samuel 14:29–33)

But seeing his father didn't tear down the wall between Absalom and David. We see no evidence that they tried to talk out their differences — only a kiss of greeting, and even that was nondescript and apparently without feeling. This perfunctory kiss pushed Absalom over the edge and set him on a collision course with his father.

Read 2 Samuel 15:1–6. Absalom had quite a sneaky plan, didn't he? He gradually stole the hearts of the Israelite people so that they would support him rather than his father. And, with these stolen hearts, Absalom forged an insurrection against the king.

> But Absalom sent spies throughout all the tribes of Israel,
> saying, "As soon as you hear the sound of the trumpet, then
> you shall say, 'Absalom is king in Hebron.'" Then two hundred
> men went with Absalom from Jerusalem, who were invited
> and went innocently, and they did not know anything. And

Absalom sent for Ahithophel the Gilonite, David's counselor, from his city Giloh, while he was offering the sacrifices. And the conspiracy was strong, for the people increased continually with Absalom. (2 Samuel 15:10–12)

As if conspiracy weren't enough of a dagger to thrust in his father's heart, Absalom twisted the blade with a shocking personal affront: he slept with his father's concubines in the sight of all Israel (see 2 Samuel 16:20–22).

Earlier Absalom had chosen the attitudes of resentment and retaliation. Later he refused to repent. Finally, he rebelled openly against his father's authority. The wall of resentment that had been built would never be torn down. The relationship between father and son would continue to deteriorate until Absalom's untimely death.

Family Huddle

During adolescence, when teens are caught in a tug of war between adulthood and childhood, they have an intense need to feel accepted. If this need isn't met at home, they'll search until their need is met elsewhere, just as Jephthah did. He found a group of friends that was every parent's worst nightmare. But he didn't care. At least these friends accepted him for who he was, and that was all that mattered to him at the time.

Many teens feel rejected at home like Jephthah because they've never been taught the difference between *acceptance* and *approval*.

When a child is being punished for something not approved by his parents, it is easy for him to get the idea that they don't like him or accept him as a person. Thus a kind of mathematical formula is implanted in the youngster:

Approval means acceptance.
Disapproval means nonacceptance or rejection.
So punishment and discipline equal disapproval and rejection. . . .

This may or may not be the parents' fault. However, if you are a parent it would be well to look closely at just how you discipline your children. Be sure to make it crystal clear that while you do not approve of what they are doing, you do accept and love them as your children. Make clear to them that your acceptance of them does not depend on your approval of everything they do.[4]

Parents, have you communicated to your children that your love for them is not based on how well they perform? If so, how? If not, why not?

_____

_____

_____

_____

This week, what can you do to make the distinction between acceptance and approval crystal clear to your children?

_____

_____

_____

_____

Two Insights for Parents to Ponder

The stories of Jephthah and Absalom leave behind two vital insights for parents today. *First: Few things are more damaging to an adolescent than rejection.* Jephthah provides a case in point. Life is hard enough for teens who are struggling with identity and self-esteem at this age, but feeling rejected makes those difficult times virtually impossible. As a parent, try to be especially affirming during your child's adolescent years. And try not to condemn. Remember, "the tongue of the wise brings healing" (Proverbs 12:18).

In what ways did the parents and families of these two young men shirk responsibility? How do you think God felt about the way Jephthah and Absalom were treated?

_____

_____

_____

_____

Did you receive mostly acceptance or rejection from your own parents? In what ways were these values expressed?

_____

_____

_____

_____

How can you express greater love and acceptance to your children?

_____

_____

_____

_____

Second: Few things are more essential to an adolescent than communication. Absalom desperately sought open communication and acceptance from his father—but he never got it. One opportunity after another slipped through David's fingers until it was too late, and he saw his son slip away forever.

How would you rate your communication with your own parents? Which issues did you feel free to discuss with them? Which issues were considered taboo?

_____

_____

_____

_____

What opportunities do you have right now to improve your communication with your parents, spouse, or children? What steps can you take in order to do so?

_____

_____

_____

_____

Adolescence is a tough time, but its hurts can be cushioned by a parent's love, acceptance, approval, and positive communication. Make a point to demonstrate these qualities to your kids, grandkids, and other young people in your life.

10

CHALLENGING YEARS OF ADOLESCENCE
(PART TWO)
2 Chronicles 34:1–7; Daniel 1:3–9

Author Jim Conway refers to the period of midlife as a "second adolescence." In developing this idea, Conway points out four major enemies of a man in the throes of that crisis.

Enemy number one: his body. He is losing his hair, his good looks, and his youthful, trim physique. Odds are good that the only thing he isn't losing is *weight*!

Enemy number two: his work. The thrill of his job has been replaced by monotony. He may feel that he's too old to change jobs or climb the corporate ladder. He often asks himself: "How in the world did I ever get stuck in a job like this?"

Enemy number three: his wife and family. His responsibilities at home make him feel trapped. Even though he wants to find a more fulfilling career, he can't leave his job because he has a responsibility to meet his family's needs.

Enemy number four: his God. The man in midlife pictures God leaning over the pulpit of heaven, pointing an accusatory finger, and preaching incriminations at him. In response, the man blames God for giving him a body with so many conflicting drives and weaknesses.[1]

Yes, "second adolescence" isn't a bad label for those going through a midlife crisis—whether they're men or women. And this term tells us a lot about how adolescents feel as well. They, too, struggle in four different areas: identity, responsibility, authority, and conformity. We covered the first two areas in the previous chapter as we studied the lives of Jephthah and Absalom. Now we'll examine the last two areas.

The Struggles of Two More Adolescents

Teenagers wrestle with a number of questions as they go through the traumatic transition of adolescence. Two of these questions concern *authority* and *conformity*. And two biblical teenagers, Josiah and Daniel, lived out the right answers.

Josiah's Struggle with Authority

Josiah came from a line of pretty rotten kings. Josiah's grandfather, King Manasseh, ruled Judah, the southern kingdom of the formerly united Israel, for fifty-five years. During most of that time, he led the people away from God. Following on the heels of Manasseh was Josiah's father, Amon. The final verses of 2 Chronicles 33 document both Amon's morally destitute character and his eventual demise.

> Amon was twenty-two years old when he became king, and he reigned two years in Jerusalem. He did evil in the sight of the Lord as Manasseh his father had done, and Amon sacrificed to all the carved images which his father Manasseh had made, and he served them. Moreover, he did not humble himself before the Lord as his father Manasseh had done, but Amon multiplied guilt. Finally his servants conspired against him and put him to death in his own house. (2 Chronicles 33:21–24)

The Jewish people then looked to Amon's son, eight-year-old Josiah, to take the throne. Remarkably, considering his family tree, Josiah developed an unswerving obedience to God. Instead of throwing off the yoke of the Lord as his father and grandfather had done, Josiah chose to follow the example of a godlier predecessor—King David. In the eighth year of his reign, while he was still a youth, Josiah began avidly to seek the God of this mighty forefather in the faith (see 2 Chronicles 34:2–3).

At the age of twenty, fresh out of adolescence, Josiah stood up and put an end to two generations of wickedness. Who or what convinced him to take such a stand? It certainly wasn't his father. God gave Josiah strength and wisdom, and the book of 2 Kings provides a clue as to another possible source of Josiah's godly courage:

> Josiah was eight years old when he became king, and he reigned thirty-one years in Jerusalem; and his mother's name was Jedidah the daughter of Adaiah of Bozkath. (2 Kings 22:1)

Usually, a new ruler's father is listed in these biblical accounts of the kings. But here, we find Josiah's mother listed instead. Why? Probably because she was the primary positive influence in his life. In 2 Chronicles 34, we see Josiah at age twenty-six, with an incredible heart for the things of God—a heart his mother probably helped cultivate. In verses 8 through 13, Josiah commissions men to repair the temple. In verses 19 through 21, we can peer through the window and discover Josiah's sensitivity to God's standards:

GETTING TO THE ROOT

Second Chronicles 34:3 says that Josiah "began to seek the God of his father David." The Hebrew word for *seek, darash,* means "to seek with care, to inquire, to search out." At the age of sixteen, Josiah made a serious, diligent search to know God. As a result of his search, he made a conscious decision to follow the Lord. His first responsibility as a godly ruler was to purify the country by eliminating idolatry. He used extreme measures to warn the people of the dangers of idol worship and to purge Judah and Jerusalem of their many altars built to pagan gods (see 2 Chronicles 34:3–5).

When the king heard the words of the law, he tore his clothes. Then the king commanded Hilkiah, Ahikam the son of Shaphan, Abdon the son of Micah, Shaphan the scribe, and Asaiah the king's servant, saying, "Go, inquire of the Lord for me and for those who are left in Israel and in Judah, concerning the words of the book which has been found; for great is the wrath of the Lord which is poured out on us because our fathers have not observed the word of the Lord, to do according to all that is written in this book." (2 Chronicles 34:19–21)

Josiah's heart broke over the things that broke God's heart: the Israelites' idolatry, wickedness, and failure to keep His statutes. The young king recognized the rightful authority of God and His Law over the nation, and he was determined to place himself and his people under that authority. He had a profound influence on his nation by destroying idols and helping to turn the people's hearts back toward God.

Parents—don't underestimate the influence of your son or daughter. If Josiah could change his nation so radically, your child can change the course of his or her nation. That potential for change starts by making a positive difference at home, school, church, work, on sports teams, at dance practice, and so on. Remind your kids to recognize God's authority, to seek Him, and to let others know the source of their faith and hope.

Daniel's Struggle with Conformity

As a young man, Daniel struggled with the question of *conformity*. Most of us remember reading the fascinating story of Daniel in the lions' den. But we tend to forget that the steel-tempered courage this godly man displayed later in his life was forged on the anvil of his adolescence. During Daniel's youth, he and his Jewish compatriots were taken captive to Babylon by King Nebuchadnezzar.

> Then the king ordered Ashpenaz, the chief of his officials, to bring in some of the sons of Israel, including some of the royal family and of the nobles, youths in whom was no defect, who were good-looking, showing intelligence in every branch of wisdom, endowed with understanding, and discerning knowledge, and who had ability for serving in the king's court; and he ordered him to teach them the literature and language of the Chaldeans. (Daniel 1:3–4)

King Nebuchadnezzar was trying to mold these young men into good Babylonian citizens. He had these monotheistic, straight-laced Jewish boys brought to the big city, where they faced enormous pressure to conform. They quickly received a crash course in the marked differences between Jewish and Babylonian life.

> The king appointed for them a daily ration from the king's choice food and from the wine which he drank, and appointed that they should be educated three years, at the end of which they were to enter the king's personal service. (Daniel 1:5)

So great was the pressure to conform that these young men were even given new names—Babylonian names (see Daniel 1:6–7). But Daniel was determined not to let his external label affect his inner commitment to God. He also made up his mind not to defile himself with the king's choice food and wine which, no doubt, had been offered to idols. So Daniel made a special request.

He sought permission from the commander of the officials that he might not defile himself. Now God granted Daniel favor and compassion in the sight of the commander of the officials, and the commander of the officials said to Daniel, "I am afraid of my lord the king, who has appointed your food and your drink; for why should he see your faces looking more haggard than the youths who are your own age? Then you would make me forfeit my head to the king." But Daniel said to the overseer whom the commander of the officials had appointed over Daniel, Hananiah, Mishael and Azariah, "Please test your servants for ten days, and let us be given some vegetables to eat and water to drink. Then let our appearance be observed in your presence, and the appearance of the youths who are eating the king's choice food; and deal with your servants according to what you see." (Daniel 1:8–13)

Fearful for his own life and skeptical about Daniel's plan, the overseer grudgingly agreed to a ten-day trial run. But amazingly, after ten days of eating vegetables and drinking water, Daniel and his friends looked more robust and healthy than the young men who had feasted on the king's food and wine.

And at the end of ten days their appearance seemed better and they were fatter than all the youths who had been eating the king's choice food. So the overseer continued to withhold their choice food and the wine they were to drink, and kept giving them vegetables. (Daniel 1:15–16)

Daniel's plan worked! He ate vegetables and drank water for the rest of his time in the king's palace, during which he had many other opportunities to demonstrate his commitment to God. Once he finished the king's course of study, Daniel graduated as valedictorian, with his three friends following right behind him.

As for these four youths, God gave them knowledge and intelligence in every branch of literature and wisdom; Daniel even understood all kinds of visions and dreams.

Then at the end of the days which the king had specified for presenting them, the commander of the officials presented them before Nebuchadnezzar. The king talked with them, and out of them all not one was found like Daniel, Hananiah, Mishael and Azariah; so they entered the king's personal service. As for

every matter of wisdom and understanding about which the
king consulted them, he found them ten times better than all the
magicians and conjurers who were in all his realm.
(Daniel 1:17–20)

What was the secret to Daniel's unique favor with the Lord? He feared
God more than he feared men. He made up his mind that he would worship
God alone, no matter the cost. He refused to defile himself with anything per-
taining to idols. And he followed through with his commitment to the Lord.

Two Practical Lessons for Parents to Ponder

The two remarkable teenagers we met in this chapter—Josiah and
Daniel—wrestled with and triumphed over the questions of authority and
conformity. From them, we can learn two practical lessons.

First: Adolescents must be given room to make up their minds. You have to
give them room to grow and succeed—even if that means that they fail a few
times along the way. Your counsel is valuable. Your support is valuable. Your
influence is valuable. But you must take your hand away at times and let your
adolescent learn to walk on his or her own two feet.

What did you learn from the lives of Josiah and Daniel that surprised you?
In what circumstances did they have to decide what to believe and devote
themselves to?

_____

_____

_____

_____

What positive influences in the lives of these two teens enabled them to
build a strong faith despite the pagan influences of their cultures?

_____

_____

_____

_____

Second: Personal convictions stand the test better than forced convictions. From
dieting to doctrinal statements, adults know the reality of this lesson. When

you make a decision based on your deep inner convictions, you will handle temptations and trials better than you would if someone else's convictions were forced on you. The same is true for teenagers. Share your convictions with them, but don't do so in a dictatorial manner. Patiently allow your teenagers to explore and develop their own convictions, and pray for them to make the right decisions. In the end, they'll thank you for it.

Parents, what are your personal faith convictions? How are you passing them on to your children?

_____

_____

_____

_____

What cultural influences and expectations can make it difficult for you at times to pass on these personal faith convictions to your children? How can you use God's Word, prayer, and other resources to battle these influences?

_____

_____

_____

_____

 ## Family Huddle

In his insightful book *The Screwtape Letters*, C. S. Lewis wrote about the process God uses to raise His children:

> He wants them to learn to walk and must therefore take away His hand; and if only the will to walk is really there He is pleased even with their stumbles.[2]

In some areas of their lives, your children will always need you to provide guidance and direction. But in other areas, you must let them try to walk on their own even if that means they'll stumble at times. When you take away your hand and give your children room to walk, they are more vulnerable to falling. But remember, they must fall before they learn to walk. And they must walk before they learn to run.

As a parent, be there to pick your kids up and dust them off when they make a mistake, but don't hold their hands through every decision in life. Give them room to change, learn, and grow. Pass on your Christian faith and heritage to your children, and give them the freedom to add their personal signature to it. As you share your convictions with them and help them learn to walk on their own, they'll develop a personal, genuine, and living faith that pleases God.

Parents, are there areas of your children's lives in which you try to lead them a little more than you should? Think through the following areas and check the ones in which you may need to help your children learn to think and act more independently. (If you need help identifying these areas, just ask your kids!) On the lines write down some specific steps you can take to accomplish your goal.

❑ Money: _____

❑ Music: _____

❑ Clothes: _____

❑ Church: _____

❑ Friends: _____

❑ Work: _____

❑ Home responsibilities: _____

❑ Relationship with God: _____

❑ Relationships with the opposite sex: _____

❑ Choices of how to spend free time: _____

❑ Hobbies and extracurricular activities: _____

As your children grow older, they'll need *more* guidance, leadership, and direction in certain areas of their lives. How can you help provide the guidance that your children need in these areas?

_____

_____

_____

We've learned quite a bit about facing the challenges of adolescence by studying the lives of Josiah and Daniel. Josiah demonstrated that he understood God's authority over himself, over the nation of Israel, and over false gods. Daniel demonstrated that he could remain true to God's standards by refusing to conform to the pagan Babylonian culture. As we apply the lessons we've learned from the experiences of these two adolescents, we can gain confidence that our children, too, can choose God's truth over lies and godly conduct over worldly living.

11

WARNING THE UNINVOLVED
1 Samuel 1–4

The deterioration of a house that once teemed with life is a tragic thing to see. Rafters sag like shoulders slumped under the burden of decades. Shingles too weary to withstand the elements create ceilings mapped with remembered rain. Windows, once bursting with morning light, are now silted over from neglect. A pall of somber, gray dust shrouds a derelict interior.

No voices emanate from the old house. No lively conversation is exchanged over the dinner table. No laughter. Only an occasional arthritic creak in the ceiling joists or an infrequent, musty wheeze from the attic . . . a nostalgic sigh for memories past.

Such a house is a sad sight.

But even more sad, more tragic, is the slow disintegration of a family. In this lesson, we'll witness one such family. And hopefully, the signs of deterioration will stand out so glaringly that they'll motivate us to make the necessary repairs before our homes suffer a similar fate.

Meet the Family

Turning back the yellowed pages of time, we come to an ancient account of a disintegrating family in 1 Samuel 1–4. No pictures of a mother are propped on this family's mantle. Instead, our eyes are drawn to the portrait of a father with his two natural sons and one adopted son.

The Father: Eli

Next to the large center portrait sit three small pictures framing separate aspects of Eli's life—professional, personal, and physical. Like many respected men today, Eli was called upon to assume a position of leadership in the community. First and foremost was his role as high priest (1 Samuel 1:9). Besides his ceremonial role, Eli served in a civil capacity as a judge—a position he occupied for forty years (4:18). Added to his professional responsibilities, Eli had the personal responsibility of being a father to his sons, Hophni and Phinehas, and his adopted son, Eli (see 1 Samuel 1).

As we view the third picture, we discover several physical qualities about Eli. In 1 Samuel 2:22, we see that he was very old and had failing vision (1 Samuel 3:2).[1] In 4:18 two more facts about Eli become clear—one negative, one positive:

GETTING TO THE ROOT

The tone of the text of 1 Samuel 1–4 and Eli's comments confirm his faith in God. In fact, Eli's name literally means "Yahweh is high" or, more likely, "Yahweh—my God" (meaning, "Yahweh is my God").

> When he [the messenger] mentioned the ark of God, Eli fell off the seat backward beside the gate, and his neck was broken and he died, for he was old and heavy. Thus he judged Israel forty years.

On the negative side, the man was severely overweight, a fact that contributed to his death. But as a positive legacy, he left behind a forty-year record of faithful service—at least in regard to his professional life. He didn't fare as well, however, in his parental responsibilities.

The Two Natural Sons: Hophni and Phinehas

Professionally, Eli's sons followed in their father's footsteps as priests (1 Samuel 1:3). Morally, however, they took a different path.

> Now the sons of Eli were worthless men; they did not know the Lord. (1 Samuel 2:12)

The remainder of 1 Samuel 2 chronicles their cavalier attitude toward sin and their cynicism toward their spiritual duties. Not only did they not know the Lord, but they disregarded the priestly customs (1 Samuel 2:13–17). And their personal lives as well as their hearts were far from God—so much so that they sinned blatantly by sleeping "with the women who served at the doorway of the tent of meeting" (1 Samuel 2:22). Catching a gust of this gossip circulating among the people, Eli confronted his sons.

> He said to them, "Why do you do such things, the evil things that I hear from all these people? No, my sons; for the report is not good which I hear the Lord's people circulating. If one man sins against another, God will mediate for him; but if a man sins against the Lord, who can intercede for him?"
> (1 Samuel 2:23–25)

Their response, however, revealed hearts that were stubborn and rebellious.

> But they would not listen to the voice of their father, for the Lord desired to put them to death. (1 Samuel 2:25)

Read Ephesians 4:18–19. How do Paul's words accurately describe Hophni and Phinehas?

_____

_____

_____

When people resist spiritual truth, that truth does not absorb into their hearts. As a result, every time they rub up against spiritual things, a callus forms on the surface instead of a fire being sparked within the heart. Every brush with their priestly responsibilities had exactly this effect on Hophni and Phinehas. They resisted truth, resented authority, and finally rebelled openly.

The same thing often happens with preachers' kids. Children who are continually exposed to churchy talk, churchy meetings, and churchy people fall prey to insincerity. Some go through the motions like marionettes on a string. They walk. They talk. They bend at the joints. They look real, but inside they have hearts of wood.

How do parents inadvertently turn their children into wooden puppets? Think of some examples of how society—or maybe even your own family—promotes calloused hearts rather than spiritual authenticity.

_____

_____

_____

The Adopted Son: Samuel

Born to Hannah and Elkanah as a special gift from God, Samuel was given to the Lord's service in grateful response to God's blessing (see 1 Samuel 1). Growing up in the home of Eli, the high priest, Samuel was raised by a foster father who was passive, aging, overweight, and rapidly losing touch with his children. On top of that, Samuel had to share the home with two rebellious older brothers.

Like a fragrant flower planted in a garbage dump, Samuel stood in stark contrast to the moral stench of Hophni and Phinehas. In this considerably less-than-ideal soil, young Samuel flourished, serving the Lord (1 Samuel 2:11) and developing into a strong young man:

> Thus Samuel grew and the Lord was with him and let none of his words fail. (1 Samuel 3:19)

This verse reveals that God protected and nurtured the tender spirit of Samuel. In the same way, He can watch over the lives of our children too. Their home may have a few weeds. Their school may be rocky soil. The moral climate around them may be diseased. God, however, is a remarkable gardener. And if we dedicate our children to the Lord, no matter what garbage dump they're in, He can put a greenhouse of grace around them—and make something fruitful of their lives.

A Fatal Progression

What was Eli's home life like? If we had lived down the street from Eli and his family, we would have had a pretty good idea of what went on there just by casting a glance in that direction.

Sins of the Sons

So shamelessly sinful were Hophni and Phinehas that they engaged in flagrant immorality at the very doorway of the tent of meeting. And "all Israel" was aware of it. So repugnant was their rebellion and so wishy-washy was their father's response that God finally stepped in with an irreversible judgment concerning Eli:

> For I have told him that I am about to judge his house forever for the iniquity which he knew, because his sons brought a curse on themselves and he did not rebuke them. (1 Samuel 3:13)

Warnings of Others

If you read through the account, you will find several messengers the Lord used to warn Eli of His impending intervention. The first warning came through town gossip about his sons that made its way back to Eli (1 Samuel 2:24).

The second warning came from an unnamed prophet:

> Then a man of God came to Eli and said to him, "'. . . This will be the sign to you which will come concerning your two sons, Hophni and Phinehas: on the same day both of them will die.'" (1 Samuel 2:27, 34)

The final warning was from God Himself in the form of a vision to young Samuel.

> The Lord said to Samuel, "Behold, I am about to do a thing in Israel at which both ears of everyone who hears it will tingle. In that day I will carry out against Eli all that I have spoken concerning his house, from beginning to end." (1 Samuel 3:11–12)

Samuel, in turn, conveyed the prophecy to Eli.

Response of the Father

Eli's way of dealing with his sons' shameful behavior had been equivalent to giving them a verbal slap on the hand—and a mild one at that.

> He said to them, "Why do you do such things, the evil things that I hear from all these people? No, my sons; for the report is not good which I hear the Lord's people circulating." (1 Samuel 2:23–24)

Eli was not only incomplete in his reproof, he even indulged his sons' fleshly appetites, as God's rebuke to him indicates:

> Why do you kick at My sacrifice and at My offering which I have commanded in My dwelling, and honor your sons above Me, by making yourselves fat with the choicest of every offering of My people Israel? (1 Samuel 2:29)

By not intervening when his sons took huge portions of meat for themselves, Eli condoned their sin. A final thing we note about Eli's response is a sort of passive fatalism.[2] Note how he resigned himself when he heard Samuel's prophecy:

It is the Lord; let Him do what seems good to Him.
(1 Samuel 3:18)

As a parent, Eli modeled passive discipline. In what ways could he have been more active in disciplining his sons?

_____

_____

_____

_____

Signs of Domestic Disintegration

In Other Words

Let me consider well how, conceivably, it could come about that Hophni and Phinehas could be born and brought up at Shiloh and not know the Lord? Well, for one thing, their father was never at home. What with judging all Israel, and what with sacrificing and interceding for all Israel, Eli never saw his children till they were in their beds. 'What mean ye by this ordinance?' all the other children in Israel asked at their fathers as they came up to the temple. And all the way up and all the way down again those fathers took their inquiring children by the hand and told them all about Abraham, and Isaac, and Jacob, and Joseph, and Moses, and Aaron, and the exodus, and the wilderness, and the conquest, and the yearly passover. Hophni and Phinehas were the only children in all Israel who saw the temple every day and paid no attention to it.[3]

—Alexander Whyte

Okay, we've met the family and observed the activity in and around Eli's home. Now the time has come to do a little evaluating. If we look closely, we will find at least four corrosive agents that eroded Eli's family life.

First: He was so preoccupied with his profession that he overlooked his family's needs. Eli's intense focus on his responsibilities as priest and judge relegated his family to a background blur. No wonder he missed his sons' faults in their formative years; they were never in focus in the first place.

Second: He refused to face the seriousness of his sons' lifestyles. When the reports of his sons' sin came to him, Eli refused to realize the gravity of the report. He must have ached inside to realize he was such a success at work and such a failure at home. Yet he rationalized away both the causes and the far-reaching consequences of his sons' actions. His sons now serve as examples to be avoided rather than emulated, trenchant illustrations of Proverbs 19:18:

Discipline your son in his early years while there is hope. If you don't you will ruin his life. (LB)

Third: He failed to respond correctly to the warnings of others. God has ways of making the blind see—even parents who are blind to their children's faults. Sometimes His ways are miraculous; often, however, they are ordinary. He may use a teacher, a neighbor, a policeman, or a grandparent to point out important matters.

How receptive are you when people issue warnings about you or your children? How respectful? How appreciative? Do you listen, or do you get defensive?

_____

_____

_____

_____

Fourth: He condoned their wrong and thereby became a part of the problem. Notice again the Lord's stinging indictment:

Why do you . . . honor your sons above Me, by making *your-selves* fat with the choicest of every offering of My people Israel? (1 Samuel 2:29, emphasis added)

Did you notice that *yourselves* is plural? Some of Eli's own problems came from adopting his sons' ways. He went from passive indifference to active indulgence. Centuries later the prophet Jeremiah, walking through the ruins of Jerusalem, lamented how sins had been passed from one generation to another.

Our fathers sinned, and are no more;
It is we who have borne their iniquities. (Lamentations 5:7)

Such is the recycled reality of sin. Yesterday's lunch, today's coffee grinds, and tomorrow's fast food wrappers will all stack up — on the family's front porch.

Family Huddle

In *Traits of a Healthy Family*, author Dolores Curran points out that Americans traditionally judged families as "good" or "bad" based on exterior signs such as affluence, church attendance, and community involvement.

> A good family . . . was one that was self-sufficient, didn't ask for help from others, supported its institutions, was never tainted with failure, starved before it went on welfare, and met all the criteria of good families as determined by community and church.
>
> People paid little attention to what went on *inside* a family—whether there was good communication, emotional support, or trusting relationships. People were only concerned about whether a family met the more obvious, visible family standards set by society.[4]

Eli was the head of a "good family." He held the top position in his field for forty years. You could imagine him as president of the Kiwanis Club in Ephraim or chairman of several prestigious boards in Shiloh. Yes sir, Eli's professional reputation was impeccable. Success at work, however, doesn't necessarily guarantee success at home. Curran continues:

> We know that families aren't good simply because of these characteristics. Yes, on the outside, a family can be successful in an American sense of the word. Its members can be achievers and possess lots of property. They can be church-goers, with the parents' marriage intact. Sadly, the family members can be miserable inside that family.[5]

Is your family a "good family"? Do you take as many pains in your parental responsibilities as you do in your housekeeping, volunteer work, or professional duties? Take a moment to evaluate the health of your home in the light of Eli's mistakes. After each question, check the box that applies to you, and write a brief summary of your thoughts.

Are you preoccupied with your profession to the exclusion of your family's needs?

❏ blindly so   ❏ partially so   ❏ not at all

Explain: _____

_____

Are you refusing to face serious problems in your children's lifestyles?

❑ wearing blinders   ❑ passively peeking   ❑ eyes wide open

Explain: _____

_____

Do you respond correctly to the warnings of others?

❑ turn a deaf ear   ❑ hear but ignore   ❑ hear and heed

Explain: _____

_____

Do you become part of the problem by condoning the wrongs your children commit?

❑ partner in crime   ❑ mildly disapprove   ❑ act in firm love

Explain: _____

_____

What happened to Eli can happen to any of us. God has recorded Eli's mistake as a danger signal for us today. Is God warning you about a certain area of your family life that needs correction?

12

WHEN BROTHERS AND SISTERS BATTLE
Selected Scriptures

In his book *The Strong-willed Child*, Dr. James Dobson comments on the scourge of sibling rivalry:

> If American women were asked to indicate *the* most irritating feature of child rearing, I'm convinced that sibling rivalry would get their unanimous vote. Little children (and older ones too) are not content just to hate each other in private. They attack one another like miniature warriors, mobilizing their troops and probing for a weakness in the defensive line. They argue, hit, kick, scream, grab toys, taunt, tattle, and sabotage the opposing forces.[1]

If your home is a war zone of sibling rivalry and you often find yourself in a foxhole waving a little white flag, this lesson may deploy the reinforcements you need to survive the battle.

Sibling Rivalry: The Biblical Record

The earliest record of a family feud is in the fourth chapter of Genesis, a grisly reminder of the aftereffects of the Fall (4:1–8). Before the Fall, the first man and woman bore God's likeness.

> In the day when God created man, He made him *in the likeness of God*. (Genesis 5:1, emphasis added)

But after the Fall, that pristine image was defaced. From then on, the image was no longer exclusively God's, but also man's; it would bear the craggy features of sin.

When Adam had lived one hundred and thirty years, he became the father of a son *in his own likeness*, according to his image, and named him Seth. (Genesis 5:3, emphasis added)

Several Examples of Sibling Rivalry

As we forge our way through Genesis, we can easily glean from its fertile chapters several examples of sibling rivalry.

Cain and Abel

By the time Adam's two sons, Cain and Abel, reached maturity, sibling rivalry was already deeply rooted. This garden was obviously one Adam had tended with a negligent hand. In fact, the rivalry became so severe that it came to a bloody resolution the day Cain killed his brother in a field (Genesis 4:8–15).

GETTING TO THE ROOT

The Hebrew for "killed" in Genesis 4:8 can be translated "slit his throat," indicating the type of raging hatred burning within Cain.

Jacob and Esau

In the home of Isaac and Rebekah, parental loyalties were divided right down the middle. Isaac favored Esau; Rebekah favored Jacob (Genesis 25:28). And it eventually tore the family apart. Although Esau was the rightful heir to the lion's share of his father's estate, his mother's favoritism led her to conspire with Jacob to deceive Isaac into conferring his blessing upon Jacob rather than Esau (27:1–27). This fanned the coals of Esau's anger, which had been smoldering for years over unresolved conflict with his brother (v. 36). In his burning rage, he plotted to kill Jacob after their father died (v. 41).

Jacob's Sons

Joseph was the favored son in Jacob's family. All the brothers knew it—and resented it. So severe was this war of sibling rivalry that they plotted to kill Joseph (Genesis 37:18). But, given a cool moment to reconsider, his hot-headed brothers sold Joseph into slavery instead (Genesis 37:28).

Three Observations

In each of the stories we've observed, hatred blazed so intensely that murderous thoughts inflamed hearts and singed consciences. Three observations emerge from what we've seen thus far. *One, no family is immune to sibling rivalry.* The homes we've looked into are some of the most prominent in the Old Testament. *Two, no family problem is unique.* Sibling rivalry weaves a stubborn thread through the centuries. And *three, no solution is easy.*

If we're honest, most of us have to admit that we had, or are still having, our share of sibling rivalry. If you could go back in time and relive those relationships, what would you change?

_____

_____

_____

_____

A Special Case Study: David's Family

David. A man after God's own heart. Giant-killer. King. Songwriter. Warrior. He was idolized by generations . . . but, as we will see, this idol had feet of clay. For although he was successful on the throne, he was a failure at home.

General Atmosphere of David's Home

David ascended to the throne when he was thirty years old and reigned for forty years (2 Samuel 5:4–5). No longer was he an obscure shepherd boy. He was now the single most important person in Israel. No longer was he surrounded by obstinate sheep, but by obsequious servants who responded to his slightest wish. No longer did he spend the night on the hard ground under the stars, but in the plush splendor of the palace.

Times had changed—and so had David. The king had become preoccupied with the throne. From breakfast until bedtime he was faced with one decision after another. He became distracted. And one of those distractions involved women.

> Meanwhile David took more concubines and wives from Jerusalem, after he came from Hebron; and more sons and daughters were born to David. (2 Samuel 5:13)

In all, David had at least eight wives, which resulted in twenty sons and a daughter.[2] Add his concubines to that number, and you have the makings of a complicated soap opera. Think of the jealousy that must have existed between the wives and concubines—not to mention between the children. Whatever problems you have at home, David had them compounded with interest!

How would you describe the health of your home growing up? Was it robust? Fair? In need of life support? In what ways, both positive and negative, have those traits been passed down to your family situation now?

_____

_____

_____

In Other Words

Polygamy is just Greek for a dunghill. David trampled down the first and the best law of nature in his palace in Jerusalem, and for his trouble he spent all his after-days in a hell upon earth. David's palace was a perfect pandemonium of suspicion, and intrigue, and jealousy, and hatred. . . . And it was in such a household, if such a cesspool could be called a household, that Absalom, David's third son by his third living wife, was born and brought up. . . .

A little ring of jealous and scheming parasites, all hateful and hating one another, collected round each one of David's wives. And it was in one of the worst of those wicked little rings that Absalom grew up and got his education.[3]

—Alexander Whyte

Specific Conflicts between the Children

Tragic conflicts within David's family grew out of the sordid soil of his past: his affair with Bathsheba and the murder of her husband Uriah (2 Samuel 11). As time passed and the children of his tangled family grew up, you can imagine the knotty circumstances that came up and the frayed feelings that resulted from family feuds (see 2 Samuel 13–18).

A brother disgraces his sister. Second Samuel 13:1–14 records the rape of Tamar, David's daughter, by Amnon, her half brother and David's son.

He [Amnon] took hold of her and said to her, "Come, lie with me, my sister." But she answered him, "No, my brother, do not violate me, for such a thing is not done in Israel; do not do this disgraceful thing! . . ." However, he would not listen to her; since he was stronger than she, he violated her and lay with her. (2 Samuel 13:11–12, 14)

Hatred festers between half brothers. Even though Tamar's loyal brother Absalom urged her to sweep the scandal under the rug, he couldn't sweep it from his heart.

But Absalom did not speak to Amnon either good or bad; for Absalom hated Amnon because he had violated his sister Tamar. (2 Samuel 13:22)

A brother murders his half brother. In the absence of a father who would deal with the crisis, hostility simmered in the pressure cooker of Absalom's heart until at last it spewed forth in an act of vengeance.

Absalom commanded his servants, saying, "See now, when Amnon's heart is merry with wine, and when I say to you, 'Strike Amnon,' then put him to death. Do not fear; have not I myself commanded you? Be courageous and be valiant." (2 Samuel 13:28)

After Absalom murdered Amnon, he then became a rebellious runaway. David had been so busy with his job that he had been remiss in his family responsibilities. But finally the problems at home got so out of hand that they intruded upon his professional life.

After Absalom murdered his brother, he knew that his father would at last have to step in and deal with the situation. So he fled. But the story doesn't stop there. Absalom rallied support to lead a conspiracy against his father in an attempt to wrest the reins of power from David's hands. But the coup failed, and Absalom was killed (see 2 Samuel 13–18). Upon hearing of Absalom's death, David was pierced to the heart with grief—we presume not only over Absalom's death, but also about his failure as a father.

The king was deeply moved and went up to the chamber over the gate and wept. And thus he said as he walked, "O my son Absalom, my son, my son Absalom! Would I had died instead of you, O Absalom, my son, my son!" (2 Samuel 18:33)

Principles for Today

Through his negligence as a father, David had sown the wind only to reap the whirlwind. But as the dust settles around the controversies that circled his throne, a few principles for today become clear—principles that can guide our homes.

Fight Passivity

The pressures of professional and personal life are so demanding that neglecting the really important things in life—like raising our families—can be easy. If families are going to hold together, parents have to roll up their sleeves and get involved. No one can be an effective parent in absentia. And no one can parent by proxy, delegating the responsibility to someone else.

Part of parenting is just showing up—being there for your kids during the trials of adolescence and being willing to ask the tough questions. Is there a thorny topic that has been long avoided but continues to fester in your family?

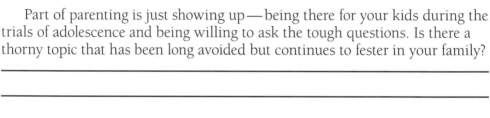

Apply Paul's words by making a commitment to address the issue today.

Communicate Clearly

Make sure you clearly communicate to your children where the fence lines are—those boundaries you've established for their protection—and delineate the consequences of climbing over those fences. And when you're setting those fence posts for your children, be sure to stabilize them in the concrete of fairness and justice so they stand straight and true.

Discipline Firmly

Once a child has crept past a fence that you've established for your home, consistent consequences must follow. Rules lose their effectiveness if they are not enforced. In turn, children lose a sense of security when they realize the fences don't mean anything.

Maintain Authority

Like Absalom, your children will often try to usurp your authority and, in some cases, overthrow it. But if you give in, it may very well result in anarchy. As long as you treat children fairly, they won't threaten your right to rule.

Parenting is not an exact science. Part of the struggle is that parents rarely pause and evaluate how they are applying biblical principles to family life. Take a moment and rate how well you are doing with each principle. Then write down at least one way you can improve in each area.

Character Trait	Poor	Fair		Great	One Way to Improve
Fight Passivity	1 2	3	4	5	
Communicate Clearly	1 2	3	4	5	
Discipline Firmly	1 2	3	4	5	
Maintain Authority	1 2	3	4	5	

Leading the Home Justly

Remember these kind of moments?

"That's mine!"
"I had it first."
"Did not."
"Did too."
"Give it back, booger face!"
Christie yells, "Mommm! Jimmy called me a booger face," then whispers, "You little worm, you're in trouble now."

Realizing his peril, Jimmy takes a deep, plaintive breath and wails, "Momma, Christie's being mean and calling me names and . . ."

Christie tries to shush Jimmy with a shove.

Jimmy counters with a hard whack to Christie's shin and a no-holds-barred bedroom brawl of pinching, punching, and hair-pulling ensues.

Finally, Mom comes in and . . .

Think back for just a moment. How would your parents have handled this?

Some parents respond to similar sibling quarrels with a detached, "I'm busy; you work it out." Others tend to threaten both parties with something worse than death if they don't "leave each other alone and be quiet!" Still others habitually blame the oldest without even bothering to look up from what they're doing.

What about your parents? Did they foster a Christlike reconciliation of fairness and forgiveness between you and your siblings? Or were you left to fight for your own rights, keeping your anger and hurt stuffed down so as not to disturb the "family peace"?

In his book *The Strong-willed Child*, James Dobson emphasizes that establishing an equitable system of justice in the home is an important parental responsibility.

> There should be reasonable "laws" which are enforced fairly for each member of the family. For purposes of illustration, let me list the boundaries and rules which have evolved through the years in my own home.
>
> 1. Neither child is *ever* allowed to make fun of the other in a destructive way. Period! This is an inflexible rule with no exceptions.
>
> 2. Each child's room is his private territory. There are locks on both doors, and permission to enter is a revokable privilege. (Families with more than one child in each bedroom can allocate available living space for each youngster.)
>
> 3. The older child is not permitted to tease the younger child.
>
> 4. The younger child is forbidden to harass the older child.
>
> 5. The children are not required to play with each other when they prefer to be alone or with other friends.
>
> 6. We mediate any genuine conflict as quickly as possible, being careful to show impartiality and extreme fairness.[4]

If you look closely, you'll find all four of our lesson's concluding principles at work in Dobson's six "laws." He and his wife were actively involved, communicating clearly, disciplining firmly, and maintaining authority.

Family Huddle

Has sibling rivalry made a war zone out of your house? Don't give up! Make it a priority to regroup and come up with some ground rules for future conflict. Set aside some time to wade through this issue that threatens to tear your home (and family!) apart.

Discuss your typical response to sibling conflict with your spouse (or a trusted friend, if you're a single parent). Then evaluate your responses in light of the four principles from our study. Are you actively involved in parenting your children? Do you communicate clearly with your kids? Is your discipline firm? Do you maintain authority while treating each child fairly?

If you don't already have a few boundaries or ground rules to govern your children's arguments, now is a good time to set some. Based on your discussion and evaluation of your responses to sibling rivalry in your home, you can outline a few "laws" to help establish a fair and just environment for your kids. Think of any new rules that need to be instituted at your house and then discuss some creative ways of enforcing your new boundaries!

13

CONFRONTING THE UNPLEASANT
Luke 15:11–32

The pain and heartache of having a prodigal son or daughter can be disorienting, defeating, and devastating for a parent. No matter how hard you try to reason with some rebellious children, they won't listen. They don't care what you think, and nothing you say or do can change that. The son who used to follow you everywhere now seems bent on following the opposite of everything you taught him. The daughter who wanted to be just like you suddenly wants nothing to do with you. What do you do when your child is too stubborn to listen? Too angry to reason with? Too old to spank?

In his excellent book *Parents in Pain*, John White provides a biblical answer.

> God's dealings with his people form a pattern for Christian parents. Like him we may eventually have to allow our persistently rebellious children to harvest the consequences of their willfulness. The time can come when we have to withdraw all support from them and oblige them, because of their own decisions, to leave home.[1]

Hard words. However, as we will see in today's study, they are wise words.

God's Response to a Rebellious Will

In the Old Testament, God took a bold, uncompromising stand on rebellion. Rebellious children were as much a problem in ancient times as they are today. The method of dealing with the problem back then, however, was considerably more decisive and final.

> If any man has a stubborn and rebellious son who will not obey his father or his mother, and when they chastise him, he

111

will not even listen to them, then his father and mother shall
seize him, and bring him out to the elders of his city at the
gateway of his home town. They shall say to the elders of his
city, "This son of ours is stubborn and rebellious, he will not
obey us, he is a glutton and a drunkard." Then all the men of
his city shall stone him to death; so you shall remove the evil
from your midst, and all Israel will hear of it and fear.
(Deuteronomy 21:18–21)

These measures appear brutal and extreme, but God viewed the sin of
rebellion as seriously as He did the worship of demons and idols: "For rebellion
is as the sin of divination, / And insubordination is as iniquity and idolatry"
(1 Samuel 15:23). At their root, both sins reject God in favor of another
master—with divination, Satan, and with rebellion, self.

The methods of dealing with a rebellious child change from the Old Testament to the New Testament. As we look at the love expressed by the father of
the prodigal son, we'll see that this love is still an example of tough love, but it
is gracious in its means and redemptive in its goal.

Christ's Parable of a Rebellious Son

Acclaimed by literary critics as the greatest short story ever written, the
parable of the prodigal son is a classic illustration of how to deal with rebellion in a Christlike way.

The Setting

The story is set in first-century Palestine, but the drama is contemporary,
re-enacted every day across the world.

And he [Jesus] said, "A man had two sons. The younger of
them said to his father, 'Father, give me the share of the estate
that falls to me.' So he divided his wealth between them. And
not many days later, the younger son gathered everything
together and went on a journey into a distant country."
(Luke 15:11–13)

Jewish law said that when a family had two sons, the elder would receive
two-thirds of his father's estate and the younger would receive the remaining
one-third at his father's retirement or death. Given the younger brother's
rivalry with his more dutiful older brother, the prodigal son undoubtedly felt
that when his father died the older brother would take the prime pastureland

and he would get stuck with the rocky back-forty. Because of these tensions at home and because of a craving to see the world, the younger son decided to leave home.

Put yourself in the father's position. How would you feel if this had been your child?

_____

_____

_____

_____

If your son or daughter were to rebel in a similar way, how would you respond to such rebellion?

_____

_____

_____

_____

_____

Did you notice the father's response to his younger son's decision? "So he divided his wealth between them." He gave no argument, no tears, and no self-righteous refusal—just the silent eloquence of his opened hand.

Deciding to let his son go was probably the most heartrending choice this father ever faced. Yet his love for his son overcame any reluctance he had. And what a doom this wandering boy was about to face.

In Other Words

Parents who are reluctant to take drastic steps should ask themselves why. Are they too scared? There is every reason to be scared. What parent is not? The thought of exposing a child to physical hardship, to loneliness and to moral temptation flies in the face of every parental instinct. . . .

Yet love must respect the dignity, the personhood of the beloved. You cannot love someone truly and deny that person the dignity of facing the results of his or her decisions. To do anything else would be to betray true love for something less than love, a "love" tainted by selfishness and weakness. Paradoxically we cannot love unless we risk the doom of the one we love.[2]

—John White

How do you know when the time has arrived to let a rebellious child walk out the door?

_____

_____

_____

_____

The Wandering

Having slipped off the yoke of domestic responsibility, the younger son trotted off to answer the call of the wild, "and there he squandered his estate with loose living" (Luke 15:13). The prodigal's eat-drink-and-be-merry life-style eventually slid him into a moral and financial pigsty.

> Now when he had spent everything, a severe famine occurred in that country, and he began to be impoverished. So he went and hired himself to one of the citizens of that country, and he sent him into his fields to feed swine. And he would have gladly filled his stomach with the pods that the swine were eating, and no one was giving anything to him. (Luke 15:14–16)

The Return

Funds exhausted, the pleasure seeker became a pauper caught in the ravenous jaws of a famine. With his poverty at its worst, he assessed his circumstances and, with his tail between his legs, slinked home.

> But when he came to his senses, he said, "How many of my father's hired men have more than enough bread, but I am dying here with hunger! I will get up and go to my father, and will say to him, 'Father, I have sinned against heaven, and in your sight; I am no longer worthy to be called your son; make me as one of your hired men.'" So he got up and came to his father. (Luke 15:17–20)

What turned this wayward son's heart toward home? The certainty of his father's love. He knew that his father would not turn him away.

Even though you may be at odds with your child, do you show love in such a way that he or she would feel safe turning back to you? Explain.

_____

_____

_____

The Response

Luke 15:20–24 resembles a climactic scene in an Academy Award-winning film. As you read, feel the emotion, the ecstasy, and the tears of joy.

> But while he was still a long way off, his father saw him, and felt compassion for him, and ran and embraced him and kissed him. And the son said to him, "Father, I have sinned against heaven and in your sight; I am no longer worthy to be called your son." But the father said to his slaves, "Quickly bring out the best robe and put it on him, and put a ring on his hand and sandals on his feet; and bring the fattened calf, kill it, and let us celebrate; for this son of mine was dead and has come to life again; he was lost and has been found." And they began to celebrate.

If the doorbell rang and you looked out the peephole to see your child who, just one year ago, had slammed the door in your face and vowed never to come home again, how would you react?

_____

_____

_____

Honestly now, if you were the prodigal son's father, would you run to this rebel before you even knew why he was returning? Perhaps he's coming to demand more money, not to ask for forgiveness. Are you willing to risk being abused by him again? Will you rush to him anyway? Don't forget, he was the one who rejected you and walked away. And now you're going to run to him? Why not wait? Or just turn away?

And will you embrace him? Can you simply forget all the hurtful words he hurled at you and cheerily dress him in your best robe? Are you eager to shower this belligerent son with kisses? Admit it, aren't you the least bit suspicious of his suddenly pious attitude? Is he really penitent? Or is he just sorry he got caught in a famine?

Preparing Yourself for the Unpleasant

The emotions described above are just a few of the hurtful feelings and thoughts that real parents of prodigal sons and daughters wrestle with. So what can you do to prepare your heart to be as forgiving and gracious as the father in Jesus's story? In *When Your Kids Aren't Kids Anymore*, Jerry and Mary White offer three helpful suggestions:

- *Stay in fellowship with God.* During traumatic times, we tend to focus exclusively on prayer and neglect feeding our spirits from the Word of God. Be sure to read consistently. And if you're having trouble concentrating, then plan to read for short periods several times a day.

- *Protect your health.* Be aware that you are more susceptible than usual to physical illness when you're stressed out. Intense emotional suffering can rob you of your sleep, your appetite, and your energy level. Learn to say no to optional activities and possibly even back away from some important commitments until the crisis is over. Pay more attention to your nutritional needs, give yourself a little extra sleep, and remember to exercise.

- *Gather a support group of close friends.* Choose those whose spiritual maturity has been proven, who are committed to prayer, and with whom you can share your hurts and hopes. This type of support and counsel is essential.[3]

Can you think of some other healthy ways to deal with your feelings? List them below.

_____

_____

_____

_____

Dealing with a Rebel

If you have a rebel at home who wants to break with the family, consider these important principles.

First: No rebellious child should be allowed to ruin a home. No rebel should be saved at the expense of the entire family. John White adds a helpful dimension to this dilemma.

> The decision to dismiss children from home should not be made either because it will work or as a matter of expediency. It should be made on the basis of justice. And justice must consider every side of the problem. Is it morally just to keep children at home when other family members suffer deprivation in one form or another because of them?[4]

If you are considering risking the doom of a rebellious child, consider again John White's advice, "We cannot love unless we risk the doom of the one we love."[5]

Before you decide to run that risk, examine your feelings that are influencing this decision. Do you feel hurt? Angry? Depressed? Are you feeling guilty for not being a better parent? Write down all of your feelings without judging whether any of them are right or wrong. Use a separate sheet of paper, if necessary.

_____

_____

_____

_____

Everyone who has dealt with a prodigal son or daughter can identify with your feelings. These feelings are intense and draining. And they make it hard to think clearly and make wise decisions. Perhaps if you wrote down your reasons for risking your child's doom, you would be able to cut through some of the emotions that are clouding your thinking.

Family Huddle

The time it takes to deal with the rebellion of one child can often leave your other children feeling overlooked. In order to get a pulse on how all your kids (even the one in rebellion) view the situation, you might try this: Take each one of them out for a pizza on separate days, and ask the pizzeria not to slice the pizza you order.

Tell your child that the pizza represents the attention (whether negative or positive) he or she and each sibling receive from you. Ask your child to divide the pizza into different sections. The size of the first section should reflect how much positive attention your child feels he or she gets. The second section should show how much negative attention your child feels he or she receives. The third piece should represent the positive attention he or she feels a sibling receives. The fourth should show the negative attention he or she thinks the same sibling gets. Have your child cut a "positive" slice and a "negative" slice for each of their siblings.

Their piece sizes will likely differ. These differences may reflect real issues, such as the extra time your rebellious child's problems take from your other children, or they may represent an unintentional favoritism your children see that you do not. While each child's "slice of attention" will vary with their needs, one child should not be taking so much attention that the others feel like they never get their slice.

After each child divides the pizza, ask him or her, "Why did you choose to cut your pieces in the sizes that you did?"

Resist the temptation to respond to your child's opinions. This time is for you to listen and learn so that you can make good decisions on how to deal with each of your kids. Your rebellious child's answers may start a dialogue that could turn them around.

If you need a neutral party to help you work through the issues raised on the pizza outings, don't be afraid to seek counseling from your church or a good Christian counselor.

Second: Principle must prevail over the person. Again, justice must rule impartially and without respect to persons—even if that person is your child. If an eternal principle is at stake, as with Eli's sons (1 Samuel 2), stand on the principle, even if that means standing against your own flesh and blood. Take a look at some further wisdom from John White.

God respected the dignity of our primal forefathers. He could have prevented their tragic disobedience and could thus have circumvented all the tragedies of human existence. He gave them a choice. They chose rebellion. He was then obliged to drive them from the garden.

If God so respects the autonomy he gave us, then we also must do the same for our children. In their earliest years they are not ready to be given full control of their lives because they are too vulnerable, too weak, too inexperienced to use it. But when the time comes, and that time must be decided by the parents as they wait on God, we must give them the dignity of letting them face the real consequences of their actions.

To do so will be painful. If ever you find yourself in that position, beware of sealing your heart in bitterness. The test of godly maturity will be to carry out the sentence combining tenderness with firmness.[6]

Third: When true repentance occurs, God honors a forgiving response and a loving welcome. "The Parable of the Prodigal Son" could perhaps be titled "The Parable of the Compassionate Father." For the son's repentance is not what overwhelms us; the all-embracing love of the father is what takes our breath away. And as the parable implies, when we joyfully embrace repentant sinners, we are most like our Father in heaven. This image not only brings sinners back to God, but also brings rebellious children back to the waiting arms of their parents.

14

FACING THE UNFORESEEN
Job 1–2

If we want to grow wise in family life, we have to give up some of our fantasies.

We would like to view the family through the sentimental wire rims of Norman Rockwell: Father is at the head of the table, carving the Thanksgiving turkey; Mother is wearing her unsoiled apron, beaming over the meal in matronly elegance; children are gathered dutifully around the table—eager, wide-eyed, and rosy-cheeked. Truly a cornucopian Thanksgiving.

In real life, though, Dad is probably snoring on the couch to the drone of football emanating from the TV. Mom is a limp dishrag after hours in the hot kitchen with a turkey that's too dry, dressing that's too soggy, gravy that's too lumpy, and rolls that are burnt on the bottom. And the kids? Well, the younger ones are pulling out each other's hair in the den. The adolescent son is locked in his room, his CD player throbbing to some alien pulse while he's chewing gum as if it were one of the four basic food groups. And the older daughter has been on the phone so long that, when she finally comes to the table, her head is fixed at a right angle.

Now *that's* real life. And taking a good look at real life is the only way to become equipped for the unforeseen.

It has been said that art often imitates life. If that's true, what movie, novel, or work of art expresses your present family reality, and why?

_____

_____

_____

_____

Life as It Is . . . Not as We Would Imagine

Cinderellas generally don't marry charming princes. Too few children can say with Dorothy, "There's no place like home." And, in the real world, father doesn't always know best. If we're going to see life as it really is, we must strip away our illusions. When you get down to basics, life consists of four key areas: people, events, decisions, and results. Let's take a look at each area and the illusions we must overcome.

People:

By virtue of the Fall, all people are sinful, selfish, and going through some kind of trouble (see Galatians 5:19–23; compare with Ephesians 4:22–32). However, we imagine that they are good, giving, and living happily ever after.

Events:

Many events that happen in our lives are unpredictable and surprising. We imagine, though, that to a large extent we can shape our destiny and predict what will happen.

Decisions:

Many decisions we make are horizontal in scope and are not necessarily aligned with biblical principles. We decide what to do based on what seems best from our earthly perspective. We often believe we have received our marching orders from God when, in fact, we may have listened to society's drumbeat instead.

Results:

The ramifications of our decisions are often far-reaching and painful to others. But we tend to imagine that we are autonomous beings and that our decisions affect only ourselves.

Life as It Was . . . Not as We Would Expect

Paging through the Scriptures, our thumb stops at the oldest book in the Bible—Job. Here we find a family that most of us would be glad to have.

An Enviable Family

Beginning in verse 1, we learn that Job was an ideal father.

> There was a man in the land of Uz whose name was Job; and that man was blameless, upright, fearing God and turning away from evil. (Job 1:1)

So widespread was Job's renown that he was recognized as "the greatest of all the men of the east." He had a wife and ten children. He was affluent. His children got along well. And most of all, Job took his relationship with the Lord seriously (see Job 1:2–5). It seems that Job's family life would have been a perfect picture for Norman Rockwell to capture on canvas. But as we will see, the colors on the palette suddenly turned dark and somber.

A Series of Calamities

Without a whisper of warning, Job's well-ordered life came crashing down around him like a house of cards. Within a span of minutes, four messengers reported to Job their devastating news.

> Now on the day when his sons and his daughters were eating and drinking wine in their oldest brother's house, a messenger came to Job and said, "The oxen were plowing and the donkeys feeding beside them, and the Sabeans attacked and took them [the animals]. They also slew the servants with the edge of the sword, and I alone have escaped to tell you." While he was still speaking, another also came and said, "The fire of God fell from heaven and burned up the sheep and the servants and consumed them, and I alone have escaped to tell you." While he was still speaking, another also came and said, "The Chaldeans formed three bands and made a raid on the camels and took them and slew the servants with the edge of the sword, and I alone have escaped to tell you." While he was still speaking, another also came and said, "Your sons and your daughters were eating and drinking wine in their oldest brother's house, and behold, a great wind came from across the wilderness and struck the four corners of the house, and it fell on the young people and they died, and I alone have escaped to tell you." (Job 1:13–19)

As we read of Job's suffering, we can share in his sorrow. What's not so easy is sharing his submissive response.

> Then Job arose and tore his robe and shaved his head, and he fell to the ground and worshiped. He said,
> "Naked I came from my mother's womb,
> And naked I shall return there.
> The Lord gave and the Lord has taken away.
> Blessed be the name of the Lord."
>
> Through all this Job did not sin nor did he blame God.
> (Job 1:20–22)

Next, Satan got another round with this battered believer and struck a vicious body blow. From head to toe, Job was afflicted with boils (Job 2:7–8). During this painful time, even Job's wife emotionally deserted him (vv. 9–10), leaving him to sift through the ashes of his spiritual confusion alone.

Though you may not have encountered the kind of extreme sorrow dumped upon Job and his family, certainly you have been through, or are presently going through, trials of your own. How have you typically responded to God when going through a crisis?

A Road to Recovery

For Job, the road to recovery was long and winding—through forty-two chapters of rugged introspection. In the first two chapters, he struggled to take four giant steps up that road.

First, he endured the agony of humanity. We find shock, grief, pain, disbelief, and panic. The text says he "tore his robe and shaved his head" and "was sitting among the ashes" (Job 1:20; 2:8). These actions were outward manifestations of his inward grief.

Second, he encountered a struggle with theology. His wife, who could not make sense of the suffering, encouraged him to "curse God and die" (Job 2:9). Surely Job wondered how God could permit such tragedy and probably questioned where God had been during his hurt, but he did not curse God.

Third, Job had to accept reality. In Job 2:10 he responded to his wife: "Shall we indeed accept good from God and not accept adversity?"

Fourth, Job found freedom from iniquity. "Through all this Job did not sin nor did he blame God" (Job 1:22). While working through grief, our tendency is to blame others, even God. But Job suspended judgment and instead submitted to God's sovereign plan.

In Other Words

God has created a world in which many more good things than bad things happen. We find life's disasters upsetting not only because they are painful but because they are exceptional. Most people wake up on most days feeling good. Most illnesses are curable. Most airplanes take off and land safely. . . . The accident, the robbery, the inoperable tumor are life-shattering exceptions, but they are very rare exceptions. When you have been hurt by life, it may be hard to keep that in mind. . . . When we are stunned by some tragedy, we can only see and feel the tragedy. Only with time and distance can we see the tragedy in the context of a whole life and a whole world.[1]

—Harold Kushner

During a crisis, which step takes the most strength for you to conquer? Is it dealing with the agony of humanity? A struggle with theology? Accepting the plight? Resisting the temptation to blame? Why?

_____

_____

_____

_____

_____

_____

_____

A Remarkable Restoration

At the end of the book, with God's restorative touch, the gaping wound in Job's life was closed and finally healed.

> The Lord restored the fortunes of Job when he prayed for his friends, and the Lord increased all that Job had twofold. Then all his brothers and all his sisters and all who had known him before came to him, and they ate bread with him in his house; and they consoled him and comforted him for all the adversities that the Lord had brought on him. And each one gave him one piece of money, and each a ring of gold. The Lord blessed the latter days of Job more than his beginning; and he had 14,000 sheep and 6,000 camels and 1,000 yoke of oxen and 1,000 female donkeys. He had seven sons and three daughters. (Job 42:10–13)

Life as It Will Be . . . Not as We Would Prefer

What we said before holds true. If we want to grow wise in family life, we really do have to give up some of our fantasies. And one fantasy that many of us refuse to let go of is that good families are trouble-free families. A trouble-free family is about as realistic as Santa Claus. What is true, Dolores Curran discovered, is that in the past, "good" families were taught to hide their problems. And this, in turn, led to the fictionalized view that "good" families have no problems.[2] Fortunately, this myth is slowly being replaced with the truth about families and problems—they're inseparable! "Good" families experience problems the same as the not-so-good ones. What makes the qualitative difference between families is how they handle them. Curran underscores this distinction with a comparison.

> The "good" family of yesterday claimed it had no problems; today's healthy family expects a variety of problems. The "good" family of the past never admitted any need for help; today's healthy family is healthy because it is able to admit to need and seek help in the early stages of a problem. In fact, it might even be said that the healthier the family today, the sooner it is likely to admit its weakness and work on it publicly, a direct turn-around from a couple of generations ago when the best families were problemless.[4]

GETTING TO THE ROOT

The Hebrew word translated "adversities" may also be translated "misery, distress, injury."[3] The word is used about twenty times to designate injury done to the body and about a dozen times to describe sorrow one may experience. Its use in Job 42:11 denotes the sum of the distressing happenings of life. This verse, which attributes Job's misery to God, poses an apparent contradiction with Job chapter 1, which attributes his suffering to Satan. Although God did not bring misery into Job's life Himself, by permitting Satan to do so, God can be looked at as ultimately sharing a degree of responsibility for what Job experienced. The difference between the responsibility of Satan and that of God was that Satan brought misery into Job's life with the intent of getting him to defect from God (Job 1:9–11). God's intent, however, was to display Job as an example of integrity and patient endurance in the midst of trials (compare Job 2:3 with James 5:11).

What about your family? Are you teaching your children to recognize and deal with problems effectively—biblically? Or are you raising them to believe in the destructive myth that good marriages and families are trouble-free ones?

One way to find the answer to these questions is by examining how you deal with family problems.

Do you expect problems and view them as a normal part of life? If not, how would you describe your attitude toward them? (For help in developing a godly perspective, read James 1:2–4 and 2 Corinthians 12:7–10.)

_____

_____

_____

_____

Are potentially serious problems dealt with early on or only after a crisis develops? Can you give an example?

_____

_____

_____

_____

How are family issues taken on? With a spirit of cooperation and confidence? Or do you refuse to face problems? Are secrecy and silence invoked as solutions?

_____

_____

_____

_____

How efficient is your family at coming to a decision? Does one person settle family problems quickly by ignoring the thoughts and feelings of others? Or do you rely on negotiation—without manipulation or competition—to arrive at a solution?

_____

_____

_____

Are you equipping your family for the unforeseen by teaching them how to deal with their problems rather than deny them?

Family Huddle

One of the best lessons we can learn as a family is that life isn't a movie, and because of sin, it can be unfair and painful. In our efforts to shield our kids from pain, we can sometimes leave them ill-prepared to face trials.

Read James 1:2–4 with your kids. As a family, discuss the following questions:

1. Will we face trials?

2. Do trials come because we've done something wrong?

3. What trials have you faced recently?

4. How have you responded to these trials?

5. How should we respond to trials?

6. Why does God allow us to go through trials?

God's Promise

As the storms of life sweep over us, we bend and sway under their force. We prefer sunshine to torrential rain and calm, idyllic days to wind-tossed nights. We prefer protection from adversity. But life continues its pelting downpour. We prefer to watch the lightning and hear the thunder from a distance. But God chooses to bring the clouds near.

We prefer to have no surprises. We prefer to live in a Norman Rockwell painting. But, despite our preferences, life remains untamed and unpredictable. Fortunately, God has given us a powerful promise:

> When you pass through the waters, I will be with you;
> And through the rivers, they will not overflow you.
> When you walk through the fire, you will not be scorched,
> Nor will the flame burn you.
> For I am the Lord your God,
> The Holy One of Israel, your Savior. (Isaiah 43:2–3)

15

ENDURING THE UNBEARABLE
2 Samuel 18–19:15

C. S. Lewis went through a long grieving process when he lost his wife to cancer. You can follow the winding road that his grief took in his book, *A Grief Observed*. In his pain, he asked searching questions about his faith:

> Meanwhile, where is God? . . . Go to Him when your need is desperate, when all other help is vain, and what do you find? A door slammed in your face, and a sound of bolting and double bolting on the inside. After that, silence.[1]

How do you typically respond when you encounter God's silence?

_____

_____

_____

_____

Sooner or later, we all encounter unbearable hardship. We wonder if the storm will ever subside, if the darkness will ever pass, if the silence will ever stop screaming. Take heart—this chapter centers on godly principles that will not only encourage us to prepare for the unbearable but also will help us to persevere through it.

When the Unbearable Is Inescapable

No one eludes the unbearable. Impossible circumstances are an inescapable thorn of a fallen world, as indicated by the life of Job, whose name has become synonymous with suffering.

For man is born for trouble,
As sparks fly upward. (Job 5:7)

Again, in Job 14:1, Job himself underscores the inevitability of human suffering.

Man, who is born of woman,
Is short-lived and full of turmoil.

When the crush of circumstances pressures us, we instinctively cry out to God for relief. David, no stranger to grief himself, recorded one such cry in Psalm 102:1–7.

Read this psalm of David and consider the following questions:

How desperate is David for relief from his hardship?

_____

_____

_____

_____

What does he ask of the Lord?

_____

_____

_____

_____

David spoke somber, anguished words from the depths of a hurting heart. When you face unbearable circumstances, are you as honest with the Lord as David was? If not, what's keeping you from crying out to Him? Pride? Anger? Self-reliance? Fear? Lack of trust? Something else?

_____

_____

_____

_____

The Unbearable Seems Unendurable

The particular unbearable situation that we'll see David endure concerned his son Absalom—a handsome, intelligent, and furiously rebellious young man.

Family Background

David sweated through much of Absalom's life, for this rebellious son brought heated turmoil to the palace (2 Samuel 13–18). Early on, Absalom became disillusioned by his father's passive response to the rape of his sister, Tamar. He later grew deceitful and finally disloyal to his father, leading a revolt against the throne. Absalom's actions left many people confused, a few people resentful, and one person in particular—Joab, David's military commander—enraged.

Absalom's Death

During Absalom's coup, David fled from the throne to spare his own life. Although the armies of the opposing sides would soon clash in the fateful forest of Ephraim, the king made every effort to spare his wayward son.

> The king charged Joab and Abishai and Ittai, saying, "Deal gently for my sake with the young man Absalom." And all the people heard when the king charged all the commanders concerning Absalom. (2 Samuel 18:5)

The battle raged between the armies of Absalom and David. But Absalom's forces were no match for the angry swords of David's mighty men (2 Samuel 18:6–7). Absalom fled through the forest in defeat, and as he did, his long, flowing hair became entangled in the branches of a large oak tree. Like a fly caught in a web, he could not extricate himself. And with the nimble promptness of a spider, Joab rushed to kill his prey.

> Then Joab . . . took three spears in his hand and thrust them through the heart of Absalom while he was yet alive in the midst of the oak. And ten young men who carried Joab's armor gathered around and struck Absalom and killed him. (2 Samuel 18:14–15)

David's Grief

Having taken refuge at the city of Mahanaim, David was anxiously awaiting news of his son's welfare. "Is it well with the young man Absalom? . . . Is it well with the young man Absalom?" he begged of Joab's messengers as they arrived (2 Samuel 18:29, 32). When the truth of Absalom's death finally came out, David's grief seemed unbearable.

> The king was deeply moved and went up to the chamber over the gate and wept. And thus he said as he walked, "O my son

Absalom, my son, my son Absalom! Would I had died instead of you, O Absalom, my son, my son!"

Then it was told Joab, "Behold, the king is weeping and mourns for Absalom." The victory that day was turned to mourning for all the people, for the people heard it said that day, "The king is grieved for his son." So the people went by stealth into the city that day, as people who are humiliated steal away when they flee in battle. The king covered his face and cried out with a loud voice, "O my son Absalom, O Absalom, my son, my son!" (2 Samuel 18:33–19:4)

In Other Words

The terrible cry that comes out of the chamber over the gate . . . is the love of a heart-broken father, no doubt. But the pang of the cry, the innermost agony of the cry, the poisoned point of the dagger in that cry is remorse. I have slain my son! I have murdered my son with my own hands! I neglected my son Absalom from a child! With my own lusts I laid his very worst temptation right in his way. . . . If he rebelled, who shall blame him? I, David, drove Absalom to rebellion. It was his father's hand that stabbed Absalom through the heart. O Absalom, my murdered son![2]

—Alexander Whyte

The Unbearable Is Not Unending

Although some pain seems unrelenting, it truly isn't. Remember Solomon's words? "There is an appointed time for everything. . . . A time to weep and a time to laugh; A time to mourn and a time to dance" (Ecclesiastes 3:1, 4). It may feel as if unbearable circumstances have wintered in your life, but remember that seasons do change. At this point in David's life, however, winter had fallen with an icy blizzard frost at the news of Absalom's death.

Joab's Counsel

Joab, who had seen the whole tragic story of Absalom's life unfold shamefully before all Israel, confronted David about the inequity of his narrowly focused grief. In bold, blunt words, he told David to face the truth and realize how his actions were affecting those around him.

Then Joab came into the house to the king and said, "Today you have covered with shame the faces of all your servants, who today have saved your life and the lives of your sons and daughters, the lives of your wives, and the lives of your concubines, by loving those who hate you, and by hating those who love you." (2 Samuel 19:5–6)

David undoubtedly felt tremendous guilt about his relationship with Absalom. As a result, his tears blurred the fact that Absalom had been bent on destroying him and any of his people that stood in the way. Enraged that David didn't see how his self-absorbed grief was demeaning the loyalty of his people, Joab lashed out.

> For you have shown today that princes and servants are nothing to you; for I know this day that if Absalom were alive and all of us were dead today, then you would be pleased.
> (2 Samuel 19:6)

Having spoken his mind, Joab then went on to give his friend a wise piece of advice: affirm the ones closest to you.

> Now therefore arise, go out and speak kindly to your servants, for I swear by the Lord, if you do not go out, surely not a man will pass the night with you, and this will be worse for you than all the evil that has come upon you from your youth until now.
> (2 Samuel 19:7)

Unbearable circumstances threw David into a vertigo of introspection. But Joab grabbed him by the shoulders, stood him firmly on the ground, and helped David to take his eyes off himself and place them on those who were in desperate need of his affirmation.

Think about a crisis you're going through now or one you've gone through recently. What things or emotions have kept you from meeting the needs of your children or other family members?

_____

_____

_____

_____

To whom can you turn to help you process your emotions so that you can help your children deal with theirs?

_____

_____

_____

David's Response

His perspective restored, the king heeded Joab's advice.

> So the king arose and sat in the gate. When they told all the people, saying, "Behold, the king is sitting in the gate," then all the people came before the king. (2 Samuel 19:8)

Does this mean David was finished grieving for Absalom? No. Was it possible to just go back to business as usual and forget about him? No.

But perhaps returning to rule the kingdom was a significant beginning step in the healing process for David, a beginning that would lead to the end of this father's unbearable pain.

Consider David's position. Though his warriors had been victorious, David felt completely vanquished by the news of Absalom's death. He couldn't congratulate his soldiers, feel joy, give direction . . . nothing. For a time, the ruler was ruled by pain and just wanted to be left alone.

Everyone who has suffered an unbearable event can empathize with David. After a crushing blow, we need time to heal before we're thrust back out to meet the needs of others.

But David was more than a father; he was a king. Thousands of people desperately needed his affirmation and leadership during that crisis. And in the midst of this painful time came the rub. On the one hand, David's pain screamed at him to shut the world out; on the other, Joab vehemently protested that he take care of his people.

Our Response

Like David, when we as parents find ourselves in unbearable situations, we face the dilemma of dealing with our own pain while struggling to help our children process their grief. How will our kids deal with their pain? How will they survive the unbearable? Surprisingly enough, many of us unwittingly leave them to sink or swim completely on their own. We often mistakenly think that children are too young to understand, or that if we can just keep things from them, they won't be affected.

Children may not share our level of understanding about the death of a parent, for example, but they do suffer the pain of loss *just as we do*. "Protecting them" by not allowing them to deal with their loss only puts barriers in the way of their healing.

If your family is in the midst of something unbearable, how can you help your children cope with their own hurt?

_____

_____

_____

Family Huddle

When your kids are facing the reality of death for the first time, it's easy to want to sugarcoat their pain for them by dismissing their serious questions with cliché answers such as, "Grandmother's in a better place." Or "Daddy's looking down on you and smiling." Rather than answering our children's profound questions too quickly or not talking about their loss at all, seize this opportunity to teach them how to turn to God when they hurt.

When you're tucking your kids in bed one night this week, ask them:

"What do you miss most about (loved one's name)?"

"If you were to send (loved one's name) a letter, what would your letter say?"

"If you could pick up the phone and tell God how you feel right now, what would you say to Him?" (After your children answer, tell them that they don't need a phone to talk to God. They can just open their mouths and start talking or talk to Him silently anytime they want to.)

After your children answer each question, you can answer them too. This will show your kids that missing loved ones and expressing grief is okay. Show them that remembering the good times is a good thing and that telling God you don't understand why your loved one is gone (or that you're angry they're gone) is okay.

How the Unbearable Can Be Endured

Let's distill the bubbling turmoil of David's life into principles that can equip us to endure the unbearable.

First: We need to be realistic. Tragedy will touch all of us in some way at some time or another. But as long as we deny that reality, we won't be prepared to handle it when it does come.

Second: We need a friend who is honest. David's life was filled with such friends, going back to Jonathan and Nathan. We all need friends who can put an arm around us while telling us the truth. And although Joab wasn't the perfect model of a friend, he was forthright with David . . . and faithful.

Third: We need a Savior who is reliable, who is the same yesterday, today, and forever (Hebrews 13:8); who will never leave or forsake us no matter what happens (Hebrews 13:5); and who will be with us always, taking our hand as we go up the hills or down through the valleys (Matthew 28:20). We have such a Savior in the Lord Jesus, who's waiting for us to turn to Him in our unbearable situations.

Finally: We need a faith that is sure, a faith that realizes all of our experiences are not intrinsically good, but in God's redemptive grace they work together for good (Romans 8:28).

Are you equipped with the necessary tools to endure the unbearable? Think about your own life and mark the appropriate boxes below.

I am realistic; I am ready to face hardship with courage.
❏ True ❏ Often true ❏ Sometimes true ❏ Not true

I encourage my friends to be honest with me.
❏ True ❏ Often true ❏ Sometimes true ❏ Not true

I make an effort to have regular time in prayer with my reliable Savior.
❏ True ❏ Often true ❏ Sometimes true ❏ Not true

I am confident that God is in control and that He is good.
❏ True ❏ Often true ❏ Sometimes true ❏ Not true

Now, take time to pray. Tell God exactly what's on your heart. He already knows what you're going through, so you don't need to sugarcoat your feelings or leave anything out. Ask Him to shore up your ability to withstand trials by giving you His perspective and His peace.

When we're shouldering unbearable circumstances, crying out to God for relief is completely natural. And when relief isn't immediate, coming to the same conclusion C. S. Lewis did—that God isn't near—is easy. But if we allow ourselves to step back and put these principles in place, we may see, as he did, that God has been working in us all along.

> Turned to God, my mind no longer meets that locked door. . . .
> There was no sudden, striking, and emotional transition. Like
> the warming of a room or the coming of daylight. When you first
> notice them they have already been going on for some time.[3]

God has His way of healing our wounds, and just as certain as there will be a time to weep, there will also be—though it may seem unbelievable now—a time to laugh again.

16

ANTICIPATING THE UNUSUAL
Genesis 6–9; Hebrews 11:7

In the field of electricity, Charlie Steinmetz had one of the greatest minds the world has ever known. In fact, he built the mammoth generators for Henry Ford's first automobile plant in Dearborn, Michigan. One day, one of those generators broke down, and the plant screeched to a halt. Unable to get the generator going again, Ford called Steinmetz.

He came and puttered around the plant for a few hours. Tinkering with a few gauges, Steinmetz turned this, adjusted that, and then threw the switch that put the massive plant back into operation. A few days later, Ford received a bill from Steinmetz for $10,000. Surprised, Ford returned the bill with this note: "Charlie, isn't this bill just a little high for a few hours of tinkering around on those motors?"

Steinmetz returned an itemized bill to Ford:

For tinkering around on the motors:	$ 10
For knowing where to tinker:	$ 9,990
Total:	$ 10,000

Ford paid the bill, probably with a smile.[1] What appeared to be of little value was in fact of greatest value—an entire assembly line depended on Steinmetz's knowledge.

We've been tinkering with the subject of how to equip families for life. But behind the scenes, tapping gauges and turning switches, is the Holy Spirit. And He knows just where to tinker, doesn't He? We've puttered around with the subjects of the unforeseen and the unbearable. Now we want to turn our attention to the unusual so we can be equipped to understand God's standard operating procedure.

God's Family . . . An Unusual Operating Procedure

God's modus operandi is the great, the unsearchable, and the miraculous, as Eliphaz confirmed in Job 5:

> But as for me, I would seek God,
> And I would place my cause before God;
> Who does great and unsearchable things,
> Wonders without number. (Job 5:8–9)

In Job 5:10–16, we note the incredible ways God works in people's lives.

> He gives rain on the earth
> And sends water on the fields,
> So that He sets on high those who are lowly,
> And those who mourn are lifted to safety.
> He frustrates the plotting of the shrewd,
> So that their hands cannot attain success.
> He captures the wise by their own shrewdness,
> And the advice of the cunning is quickly thwarted.
> By day they meet with darkness,
> And grope at noon as in the night.
> But He saves from the sword of their mouth,
> And the poor from the hand of the mighty.
> So the helpless has hope,
> And unrighteousness must shut its mouth.

God's workings give hope to the lowly and defenseless, while dumbfounding the high and mighty. The New Testament counterpart to this passage is Romans 11:33.

> Oh, the depth of the riches both of the wisdom and knowledge
> of God! How unsearchable are His judgments and unfathom-
> able His ways!

Stop for a minute and think through the Bible. God's Word is just bursting at the seams with the incredible ways God works. The parting of the Red Sea. Manna from heaven. The pillars of cloud and fire to guide Israel in the wilderness. Jericho's wall. The Virgin Birth. Turning water into wine. Feeding the five thousand. Healing after healing. The Resurrection. The indwelling of the Holy Spirit. The list goes on and on. God still desires to do the unusual and the unsearchable . . . but are we open to that? Are we ready? Are we willing to let Him work in unusual ways?

Noah's Family . . . A Study in Surprises

Though far from perfect, Noah's family stood out in its day. They were open, ready, and willing to be a part of God's plan, even if that plan seemed highly unusual.

Difficult Times in Which to Live

Noah and his family grew up in an ungodly culture. Depravity paraded on the streets in a raucous Mardi Gras of immorality.

> Then the Lord saw that the wickedness of man was great on the earth, and that every intent of the thoughts of his heart was only evil continually. The Lord was sorry that He had made man on the earth, and He was grieved in His heart. . . .
>
> Now the earth was corrupt in the sight of God, and the earth was filled with violence. God looked on the earth, and behold, it was corrupt; for all flesh had corrupted their way upon the earth. (Genesis 6:5–6, 11–12)

Lest we place too much emphasis on the environment's role in shaping character, note that in the midst of this social cesspool there arose an unsoiled saint.

> But Noah found favor in the eyes of the Lord.
>
> These are the records of the generations of Noah. Noah was a righteous man, blameless in his time; Noah walked with God. (Genesis 6:8–9)

Righteous before God and blameless before others, Noah was like a salmon swimming upstream against the swift and sordid currents of his culture.

What set Noah apart from the other people of his time? What does the life of a man or woman who walks with God in the midst of a corrupt culture look like?

_____

_____

_____

_____

A Frightening Prophecy and a Creative Plan

In Genesis 6:7, 13, and 17, God unveiled a sobering glimpse of the brimming cauldron of His wrath.

> The Lord said, "I will blot out man whom I have created from the face of the land, from man to animals to creeping things and to birds of the sky; for I am sorry that I have made them." . . .
>
> Then God said to Noah, "The end of all flesh has come before Me; for the earth is filled with violence because of them; and behold, I am about to destroy them with the earth. . . . Behold, I, even I am bringing the flood of water upon the earth, to destroy all flesh in which is the breath of life, from under heaven; everything that is on the earth shall perish."

But before His wrath spilled over to inundate the world, God arranged a creative plan of deliverance for righteous Noah.

> Make for yourself an ark of gopher wood; you shall make the ark with rooms, and shall cover it inside and out with pitch. This is how you shall make it: the length of the ark three hundred cubits, its breadth fifty cubits, and its height thirty cubits. (Genesis 6:14–15)

Once constructed, this ark would measure 450 feet long, 75 feet wide, and 45 feet high, and would have the same volume as 522 livestock railroad cars.[2]

God's request was highly unusual because *it had never rained before*, let alone flooded (Genesis 2:5–6). But, while a reprobate world scorned, God was in the process of saving a remnant—a small portion of humanity who still believed in Him, still loved Him, and still served Him (6:18–21).

Obedience, Deliverance, and Blessing

Noah obeyed God and built the ark (Genesis 6:22), a task that took his family 100 years to complete (compare 5:32 with 7:6). At last the day came that would seal the fate of a decadent world.

> Then the Lord said to Noah, "Enter the ark, you and all your household, for you alone I have seen to be righteous before Me in this time." (Genesis 7:1)

Again Noah's obedience is underscored: "Noah did according to all that the Lord had commanded him" (Genesis 7:5). For forty days and forty nights the rains fell (7:12). Yet, in the midst of this destruction, God's deliverance was at work, saving everyone and everything in the ark. When the water dried up, Noah built an altar to thank God for taking them safely through the flood (see 7:23 and 8:20–21). And God responded with His blessing.

> And God blessed Noah and his sons and said to them, "Be fruitful and multiply, and fill the earth." (Genesis 9:1)

Because of his incredible trust in God, Noah is enshrined in the Hall of Faith of Hebrews 11.

> By faith Noah, being warned by God about things not yet seen, in reverence prepared an ark for the salvation of his household, by which he condemned the world, and became an heir of the righteousness which is according to faith. (Hebrews 11:7)

God asked Noah to believe and to do some pretty incredible things, yet he trusted, and he obeyed.

By faith, Noah believed God's warning. By faith, he obeyed by building the ark. And by faith, he became an heir of righteousness. Is God asking you to believe and do some pretty incredible things right now? To trust Him when those around you are calling you a fool for doing so? Remember, they called Noah a fool too. And while he was on his way to Hebrews 11, they were left behind.

What is God calling you to do or believe that the watching world would call foolish?

_____

_____

_____

_____

Why is it tempting to listen to the world's opinions rather than to follow God?

_____

_____

_____

_____

How will you explain to your children your choice to tune out the noise of the world and instead listen to God's voice? How will you explain your choices to your unbelieving friends?

_____

_____

_____

_____

Don't miss the chance to let those who are watching you build your ark on a sunny day meet God through you. Every time we choose to follow God, we have an opportunity to invite others to come with us.

In Other Words

Christians are to be good news before they *share* the good news. The words of the gospel are to be incarnated before they are verbalized . . . The music of the gospel must precede the words of the gospel and prepare the context in which there will be a hunger for those words.[3]

—Joseph Aldrich

A living mystery. That applied to Noah all right, a man who lived his life in such a way that it could only make sense if God existed. How about your life? Are you a living mystery? Or have you played it safe, hedging your bets to make sure you won't look like a fool? Do people look at your life, as they did Noah's, and scratch their heads, wondering what in the world you're up to now? If not, maybe you're not building a big enough boat. Maybe you're not trusting God for the unusual.

Your Family . . . Some Practical Suggestions

Noah and his family model the importance of following God, even if the path of obedience is highly unusual, even if the road is steep, the way rocky, and the visibility poor. These suggestions will better equip your family for the unusual.

First, remind your family that the unusual is God's standard operating procedure. He may use the unusual to show Himself and His provision to you.

Second, keep in mind that He is still looking for families who will model His message. He is eager to add more names to the list of faithful who have followed Him throughout the ages. Maybe your family's choices to buck the culture and instead follow God will influence others to do the same.

Family Huddle

Take some time as a family to record the times that God's unusual standard operating procedure has affected your family history. Perhaps you'll recall the time He asked you to trust Him for financial provision when the world was telling you to accrue more debt. Or maybe you'll remember the day you and your spouse prayed and sought counsel in order to work out your problems rather than throwing in the towel on your marriage.

Use a special journal or photo album to keep a living history of the times God has called your family to trust Him. Allow everyone in the family to place entries in this book to record God's call and the response of each family member. Pretty soon, your clan will have a living Hall of Faith like the one recorded in Hebrews 11 that shows how responding to God in faith has forever changed your family.

Third, fight the tendency to prefer security over availability and to prefer today's comfort over tomorrow's challenge. Our culture tells us to embrace the ease of comfort and avoid the hardship that can come with challenges, but our God calls us to follow Him even when His way seems difficult. Though following Him may not always be the easy choice, He promises that it will always be His best for us.

Take a moment to look back over the past year. In the previous twelve months, have you let your own desire for security block your availability to God? Before answering, consider your financial choices, the way you and your family have spent your time, and the goals you have pursued. The things you've thought about most and the ways you've spent your family's time and money serve as good indicators of the focus of your heart.

Finally, listen to your children when they urge you to do the unusual. Remember, God often speaks through them too. After all, the children were the ones who recognized Jesus as the Messiah and sang His praises while the adults blindly criticized from afar (Matthew 21:15–16).

What have your kids urged you to do for God that you've thought was only a childish whim or adolescent dreaming? What might happen if your family followed your kids' ideas?

In the twentieth century alone, many men and women have accomplished great works by faithfully following God's leading in the unusual. Some of these modern-day Noahs, however, made one grave mistake in building and launching their ministries—they forgot their families.

Noah made many sacrifices to build the ark, but the one thing he didn't sacrifice was his family. Under his supervision, they worked together to build the ark, and together they watched God close the door behind them when the rains began.

Remember, God's will is not that you sacrifice your family in order to accomplish the unusual (compare Ephesians 6:4; 1 Timothy 3:1–5; 5:8). Challenge your family members and show them how they can work by your side as you pursue your ark of the unusual.

17

ACCEPTING THE UNDENIABLE
Selected Scriptures

If only.

Those two words, along with slumped shoulders and downcast eyes, so often follow us through life. "If only I had known. . . . If only I could take back what I said. . . . If only I could undo what I did. . . ."

If only.

Words of regret. Words of shamed remembrance. Words that admit we've blown it.

The discouraging thing about studying Scripture is that we see how many mistakes we've made in life. Intellectual mistakes. Spiritual mistakes. Conversational mistakes. The list goes on and on. But no mistakes are as painful as people mistakes, especially mistakes made with people we love — like our children.

Although turning back the clock is impossible, we can turn the negative memories of those mistakes into something positive.

When was the last time you blew it with your children? What was the situation, and what would you have done differently?

_____

_____

_____

_____

Inescapable and Painful Realities of Humanity

"To err is human" is a shopworn sign we could all hang over our lives. No matter how much we regret them, mistakes are an inescapable part of our humanity. Humans are all imperfect, including our offspring. We cannot change the past, including the way we raised our children. And we are personally responsible for our own mistakes—even the innocent ones. A hastily woven blanket of rationalization can cover our mistakes with flimsy excuses, but it doesn't make them disappear. And an accusing finger pointed at others doesn't diffuse the blame; it only confuses it.

Guidelines for Recovery and Renewal

So how do we recover from the mistakes we've already made? For an alcoholic, the first step of recovery is to look people in the eye and say: "Hello. My name is so-and-so. I'm an alcoholic." Parents also need this kind of honesty and forthrightness when they take that first step on the road to recovery after blowing it with their children. Several guidelines will help you choose the right path to renewed relationships with your children.

Things That Won't Help

Admitting your mistakes is an important step to overcoming them. But it won't help to think: "It's all my fault." Problems in relationships are seldom just one person's responsibility, even in parent-child relationships.

In Other Words

Parents are admonished to bring up children properly. Children are admonished to respond wisely to parental correction. If both play their part all will be well. But it takes a parent-child team working in harmony to produce this happy result.

You cannot ever control another human being, even if that human being is your own child.[1]

—John White

Parenting, at its best, is a complex and demanding task. At its worst, being a parent presents no-win situations that can produce the most frustrating guilt trips in all of life. Although we are imperfect parents, we are not the antecedent to all of our children's problems. Even God, the only perfect parent, has to manage considerably less-than-perfect children.

Another thing to avoid is misunderstanding the intent of various portions of Scripture. God's Word is the light that guides our way, but the Bible isn't Aladdin's lamp. We can't rub it three times and—abracadabra!—expect a genie to appear and grant us our wishes. The Bible contains both promises and principles. Proverbs 22:6 is a good case in point.

> Train up a child in the way he should go,
> Even when he is old he will not depart from it.

This verse usually holds true. But God gave it to us as a principle, not as an absolute promise. As we all know, no matter how well-taught they were in their youth, some children become prodigals.

A good way to keep from making absolutes out of general principles is to avoid shackling them to words like *never* and *always*. Another way is to distinguish biblical principles from promises. Promises are invariably so; principles are usually so.

Take some time to look up the verses below. In the columns to the right, indicate whether the verse is a promise or a principle and then explain how you can apply the verse to your family life.

Verse	Principle or Promise?	Application to My Family
Proverbs 13:24		
Proverbs 30:33		
Matthew 6:25–26		
John 10:27–29		
Hebrews 12:5–11		

Things That Will Help

In principle, Isaiah 58 presents a correlation between how a nation can recover from mistakes and how a parent can do the same. Although Isaiah wrote thousands of years ago to the Jewish nation, his words are as applicable today as they were the day they were written. The context of the passage finds Judah's relationship with God in ruins. God counsels the people not to simply go through the motions of fasting and repentance. Rather, He recommends true fasting.

> Is this not the fast which I choose,
> To loosen the bonds of wickedness,
> To undo the bands of the yoke,
> And to let the oppressed go free,
> And break every yoke? (Isaiah 58:6)

God was looking for soft hearts that would care about what He cared about, which would provide the bedrock upon which He would rebuild their lives. From Isaiah 58:7–12 we can fashion five important truths that will lay a sturdy foundation for the recovery and renewal of our relationship with our children.

First: Humble yourself. God wanted to see humility of heart, a spirit that would extend a caring hand to the hungry and the homeless.

> Is it not to divide your bread with the hungry,
> And bring the homeless poor into the house;
> When you see the naked, to cover him;
> And not to hide yourself from your own flesh?
> Then your light will break out like the dawn,
> And your recovery will speedily spring forth;
> And your righteousness will go before you;
> The glory of the Lord will be your rear guard. (Isaiah 58:7–8)

The biggest obstacle to humility is pride. Pride keeps our necks stiff and our backs straight, a posture that has trouble bending before God and genuinely reaching out to others. By way of application to the family, if we lower ourselves in humility and admit our failure to our children, we will have taken a giant step toward recovery. As you relate to your children, is your attitude so fixed and rigid that you can't get down on their level?

Second: Pray. The result of a humble, repentant heart is obedient action. And the result of obedient action is heard prayer.

> Then you will call, and the Lord will answer;
> You will cry, and He will say, "Here I am." (Isaiah 58:9)

Our prayers are hindered when we are out of fellowship with God and each other (see 1 Peter 3:7). And we can't afford to have that happen, because praying for our children is vital to any hope of rebuilding the broken walls in our relationships.

Third: Remove the yoke. The next bit of rubble the people had to clear away from their spiritual lives is found in the second half of Isaiah 58:9.

> Remove the yoke from your midst,
> The pointing of the finger and speaking wickedness.

Do you want to break the constricting yoke that chafes your relationship with your children? Then ease the heavy load of blame from their shoulders—withdraw the pointing finger and stop hurling accusations. Change your attitude . . . and your heart.

Fourth: Make yourself available and vulnerable. God tells us that He will bless us and meet our needs when we give ourselves to meeting the needs of others.

> And if you give yourself to the hungry
> And satisfy the desire of the afflicted,
> Then your light will rise in darkness
> And your gloom will become like midday.
> And the Lord will continually guide you,
> And satisfy your desire in scorched places,
> And give strength to your bones;
> And you will be like a watered garden,
> And like a spring of water whose waters do not fail.
> (Isaiah 58:10–11)

Are you available to your children when they hunger for attention? Are you supportive when their esteem is afflicted? Great encouragement can be found in these verses for all of us who've blown it. No matter how dark the shadows that stalk us from the past, those haunting memories can't outshine the light of God's grace. He can take a desert of conflict and transform it into a verdant valley of peace.

Fifth: Trust God to bring the changes. Although the people's relationship with God was in a ramshackle condition, it could still be rebuilt. It would have to be done from the ground up, but God would give His people the strength to do it.

> Those from among you will rebuild the ancient ruins;
> You will raise up the age-old foundations;
> And you will be called the repairer of the breach,
> The restorer of the streets in which to dwell. (Isaiah 58:12)

The rubble of a ruined relationship with a child often takes no less work to rebuild—sometimes it takes more because our children are not always as ready to forgive as God is. However, when your children see you investing your time in rebuilding the ruins of your relationship, they have a good chance of changing their perspective of you. They will begin to see you as a repairer and a restorer instead of a destroyer. In His time and in His way, God can rebuild relationships and restore foundations that were torn down years ago.

Turn Regret into Reconciliation

Isn't it true—we all want the other person to apologize first before we magnanimously offer an apology? That is, of course, if we had planned to apologize at all. It may be that after we finish comparing our "harmless mistakes" with their "grossly unfair sins," we may smugly decide we shouldn't have to apologize about anything!

We learned that the first step on the road to recovery is forthrightly and honestly admitting *our* mistakes—not our adversary's. Our focus isn't to be on comparing sins, but rather on confessing them.

Have you blown it with one of your children lately? Are you willing to admit your mistakes and seek reconciliation, or are you waiting, keeping yourself busy comparing sins? Use the space provided to write what you think needs to be confessed to your child and when you plan to do it.

What I need to confess:

_____

_____

_____

_____

When I plan to do it:

_____

_____

_____

Essentials along the Way When Seeking to Rebuild

Remember, restoring relationships doesn't often come quickly or easily. Solomon wrote of this truth in Proverbs 18:19:

> A brother [or child] offended is harder to be won than a strong city,
> And contentions are like the bars of a citadel.

Our mistakes may have caused genuine offense and may have hurt our children deeply. Their resistance and reluctance to respond to us—and their defensiveness—are like the strong bars of a well-guarded castle. In other words, they may not jump at the chance to forgive us right away, which brings us to three essentials to keep in mind when we attempt the delicate work of rebuilding.

- *Have the right motive.* Be honest—don't manipulate your child.

- *Be patient.* It took time for your relationship with your child to come to its current state. Realize that the rebuilding process could take just as long—and take much more work.

- *Do it all in God's strength.* Invariably, God's strength manifests itself in our weakness (2 Corinthians 12:9–10; Philippians 4:13).

If one thing is constant about parenting, it's making mistakes. But that doesn't mean we are all fated to be wretched parents. Some moms and dads obviously manage to do a great job of parenting despite their blunders. How do they do this? How do they preserve a good relationship with their children and teach them the right things in the midst of blowing it over and over again?

Perhaps the answer can be found in your own life. Can you remember a time when one of your parents badly wronged you but later humbly asked for your forgiveness? If so, think about it for a moment. Relive that moment when he or she came to confess the wrong and ask for forgiveness.

_____

_____

_____

_____

If you've experienced this, it had a profound impact on you, didn't it? All the sermons on humility combined probably couldn't match the power of that one example. It affirmed that person's integrity, it restored and enhanced your respect for that parent, and it strengthened your ability to be compassionate and forgiving.

Admitting mistakes, especially to our children, is not easy. But when we do, we model such godly traits as humility, integrity, and Christlike love, which have great power to restore relationships and mold character.

Of course, if your parents refused to admit their mistakes, then you may have learned powerful lessons in the deceitful art of *denial* ("It wasn't my fault"); *blame* ("She did it first"); and *rationalization* ("He made me"). Over time, the unresolved wrongs in such relationships stack up to form barriers, blocking almost every level of communication except the most superficial.

If you're serious about seeking forgiveness and healing the wounds in your relationships with your children, identify the one principle that you find to be your greatest hurdle to reconciliation. Then pray that God will give you the strength to clear it and start fresh with your family member.

- ❏ Put away your pride and humble yourself
- ❏ Pray about it
- ❏ Remove the yoke of blame
- ❏ Make yourself available and vulnerable
- ❏ Trust God to bring the changes

Family Huddle

As parents, we need to show our kids that, although we are the grown-ups, we're not perfect. When we ask for their forgiveness, they will learn that forgiveness brings healing. In turn, they will be more likely to acknowledge the wrong they've done to others. After dinner tonight, ask your kids the following:

1. Have I done anything to hurt you this week? If so, what?

2. Have any of my decisions been unfair this week? In what way?

3. Are there words I've said this week that have made you angry or sad?

4. Have I not trusted you when I should have this week?

If your kids' answers reveal that you've wronged them, ask them to forgive you. Always be as quick to go to your kids and ask for their forgiveness as you would want them to be when they need to ask for yours.

Though it may seem easier to deny the fact that we've hurt our children, to blame others for our blunders, or to rationalize our wrongdoing, it really isn't. When we refuse to honestly admit to our children our mistakes and ask for their forgiveness, our pride adds another brick to the wall of resentment between us and our kids. If we refuse to knock the wall down, then we'll leave our children—the ones we've poured our lives into—alone on the other side of the wall, wondering why we held onto our pride instead of letting it go and reaching out to them.

18

RELEASING THE REINS
Ephesians 4:11–16

Of all God's creatures, humans have the hardest time releasing their offspring. Bears have no trouble saying good-bye to their cubs. Wolves don't slump into depression once their litter is weaned and leaves home. And eagles literally push their eaglets out of the nest.

So why do humans instinctively want to hold on to their children? Why do we take so long to release the reins? Why do we try to keep our children in the nest when they should be out flying on their own?

Maybe we fear that they're not quite ready for the real world. Maybe we feel we haven't done an adequate job of preparing them to face life. Unfortunately, keeping them in the nest offers no assurance that they will develop stronger wings. In fact, children who are coddled too long in the nest may never develop the strength to fly on their own. They grow into adults who lack self-confidence and the ability to think and act independently.

Releasing the reins allows children the opportunity to stretch their *own* wings. Sitting back and watching them leave is difficult, as they perch precariously on the edge of the nest, wings fluttering uncertainly. But that time of departure can be easier if we understand the process.

Progressive Cycles in Families

The first step in preparing to release your child is understanding the cycles that most families go through. Like the seasons, these stages overlap to a certain degree and vary in length, but basically they follow a definite progression.

Stage one: *Family founding.* This begins with the wedding and continues through the birth of the first child.

Stage two: *Childbearing.* This starts with the birth of the first child and lasts until the final child enters school.

Stage three: *Child rearing.* This lasts from the time the first child enters school until the final child enters college or leaves home.

Stage four: *Child launching.* Beginning with the first child's departure from home, this stage lasts until the final child leaves.

Stage five: *Empty nest.* All the children have left home.

Each of these stages has its own struggles, but perhaps none is as heartrending as the fourth. Mothers who have wrapped their entire lives around their children sometimes become devastated when the children leave home. Fathers who have smothered their children with control may become resentful when their authority is eclipsed by the children's independent steps toward freedom. But launching children from the nest needn't be a traumatic experience if certain principles are taken into consideration.

What stage of life is your family in? As your family transitions from one stage to the next, are you preparing your heart to release your children gradually so that they will be ready for the next stage and you will be ready to let them enter it?

Think about one area in which you want your child to have matured in the next two years. What can you do in the next twenty-four months to be preparing your child to take hold of the reins more tightly in this area?

As parents, we're often tempted to do things for our children because we think we're helping them. When we insist on coordinating our four-year-old's clothes because her selection doesn't match or when we do our middle schooler's science project for him to help him out, we're really hindering them from developing the skills they need for independence. When we come alongside our children, we should assist them rather than assuming responsibility for their tasks. Even if the outfit is atrocious or the erupting volcano merely bubbles, our children gain confidence and self-assurance as they do tasks themselves. Their first tries may not be perfect, but every time they do another task on their own, they will strengthen their wings a little more.

Preparation and Principles for Child Launching

The primary application in Ephesians 4 deals with the growth and development of our heavenly family—the church. However, we can also apply these principles to the growth and development of our earthly families. Verses 11–12 describe the role and responsibility of those called to lead God's family.

> And He gave some as apostles, and some as prophets, and some as evangelists, and some as pastors and teachers, for the equipping of the saints for the work of service, to the building up of the body of Christ. . .

Just as God appointed leaders for the church, so He has designated parents to lead the family. Their job description has a single focus: to equip and build up their children so that they might successfully survive the seasons of life. The following principles will help prepare your children—and you—for that time of release.

Principle one: Keep your role uppermost in mind. Your role is equipping children for life—not keeping them near your side. You are to prepare them for adult life, as church leaders prepare their members.

> . . . for the equipping of the saints for the work of service, to the building up of the body of Christ; until we all attain to the unity of the faith, and of the knowledge of the Son of God, to a mature man, to the measure of the stature which belongs to the fullness of Christ. (Ephesians 4:12–13)

Ultimately, church members must be loyal not to their leaders but to the Lord. The same is true of the parent-child relationship. Verse 12 describes the process of equipping, which leads to service, which, in turn, leads to the overall health and growth of the body of Christ. In this process, parents, like church leaders, can know that they're on the right track when they see their children growing in unity, increasing in the knowledge of God, becoming mature, and developing Christlike character.

If we hold our children too closely and fail to equip them for life, are we looking out for their best interests? What motivates us to hold them too close? What are the results if we hold them too close?

Sometimes we think we're loving our children when we're really smothering them with our own selfish desires and agendas. Remember that our job as parents is to grow a child into a responsible and independent adult—not into someone who is chained to our expectations or visions for their future.

Principle two: Watch for signs of maturity and reward the result. Maturity unfolds at a different rate and fashion with each child. Like the blooming of a flower, growth shouldn't be forced. However, as each petal of maturity unfurls itself, parents should recognize the progress and reward it appropriately.

On the road to maturity, our children may take an occasional detour or hit a pothole. When that happens, we, as parents, need to be there . . . to guide, to encourage, and to help them find their way.

Recall the last pothole your child hit. How did you handle his or her "bad driving?" Did your response guide your child toward maturity or did it label him or her as childish?

While our children's irresponsible decisions do show their immaturity, we should use those poor decisions as an opportunity to exhort our children to grow rather than as a means of discouraging their maturity.

> Speaking the truth in love, we are to grow up in all aspects
> into Him, who is the head, even Christ. (Ephesians 4:15)

Love doesn't stand at the side of the road in silence. Nor does it shout, "I told you so!" Instead, love speaks the truth in a constructive and gentle manner.

Principle three: When an older child reverts to childishness, confront the behavior with honesty and love. The Bible doesn't take a sink-or-swim approach to parenting. Parents aren't supposed to stand on the riverbank passively watching their children wade into deep and treacherous waters. Instead, we should follow Proverbs 27:5–6, which gives some helpful advice for what to do when our children make mistakes.

> Better is open rebuke
> Than love that is concealed.
> Faithful are the wounds of a friend,
> But deceitful are the kisses of an enemy.

Principle four: Help your children discover and develop their own individuality, respecting it in a context of love. Turning our attention again to Ephesians 4, we note that each member of Christ's body is unique and important.

> The whole body, being fitted and held together by what every
> joint supplies, according to the proper working of each indi-
> vidual part, causes the growth of the body for the building up
> of itself in love. (Ephesians 4:16)

When you treat your children as individuals who have been uniquely crafted by God for a special place in the body of Christ and in society, their sense of self-worth is enhanced. Then they can see themselves as being "fearfully and wonderfully made" instead of being mass-manufactured on some celestial assembly line.

Two Rules to Remember

As we conclude this subject of releasing the reins, a couple of rules will help us let go.

Encourage Growth Rather Than Tolerate It

Growth is evidence of life. Continued growth produces both maturity and stability, two qualities David prayed about for his children.

> Let our sons in their youth be as grown-up plants,
> And our daughters as corner pillars fashioned as for a palace.
> (Psalm 144:12)

Release Continually, Not Suddenly

Every year, release your grip a little bit more. In fact, you should begin releasing your children as soon as they are born. Remember, God has loaned your children to you for just a few years. They are borrowed—not owned—treasure. You are a trustee of that treasure, not the titleholder. And, when releasing your child seems like an emotionally exhausting task, remember that God the Father set the example by releasing His only Son from the nest of heaven into our world.

Part of releasing our children involves letting them be who God designed them to be, even when they differ from us. How are your children different from you? What differences are you encouraging? What are you not encouraging? Why? Are these moral issues or merely personal tastes?

_____

_____

_____

_____

_____

How might your desires for your children to be like you make them more like Christ?

_____

_____

_____

How might your desires for your children to be like you conflict with the way God designed them?

_____

_____

_____

Rather than trying to dictate exactly how their children will be, *healthy* parent-child relationships demonstrate a deep respect for the unique experiences of each child. In such an environment, children are allowed to see things differently from one another—and from their parents—and still be accepted. Therefore, they express themselves more clearly and openly and take responsibility for their thoughts, feelings, and actions.

Unhealthy parenting seeks to maintain strict control of a child's behavior and thoughts, while harboring mistrust of a child's feelings and drives. *Control* is the key word, allowing only limited growth of the child's personal bents. Any thoughts or feelings that violate the family rules are simply not allowed. Thus, children learn to suppress and deny certain feelings and thoughts in order to be accepted by their parents.

When unhealthy parenting goes to the extreme, *sameness* is the overriding characteristic. These parents view individuality in their kids as a personal rejection and therefore seek closeness through sameness. They show no respect for what their children naturally think or feel by constantly telling them what they should think and feel. All boundaries of uniqueness and self-respect are blurred in favor of enforcing a family sameness that is almost impossible to escape.

Are you allowing your children to see things differently and still be accepted? Can you give some specific examples?

_____

_____

_____

Family Huddle

Your teens may start to ask for the reins in many areas at once, and you may find yourself holding on too tightly or losing your grip in an area where your guidance is desperately needed. To assess your grip, take time to talk to your teen about his or her needs. Become sensitive to times during the day or week when your teen seems open and more conversational. Then, talk through the following questions:

1. Which of the following best describes how I usually relate to you?

   a. A compass that guides you, but lets you choose the route
   b. A map with several viable routes marked
   c. A set of driving directions outlining one optimal route
   d. A chauffer who drives you on a predetermined route

2. Which option in question one looks most appealing to you? Why?

3. If you had to pick one area in your life where you'd like more freedom, what would it be? Why?

4. If you had to pick one area in your life where you want to be more responsible, what would it be? Why?

Shaping God's Children

Rather than molding your kids into your image of the perfect child, develop them to be the person God designed them to be. Though His vision for their futures may not be identical to yours, remember that while you're dreaming of your child's tomorrow, God is orchestrating eternity. He's given you your kids for a time. They are His for all time.

Once you've released your children to fly completely on their own and the empty-nest days come, you could retire and spend your days hitting eighteen holes on the golf green or shopping 'til you drop. Or you could use the wisdom you've gained through your years in the marriage and family trenches to encourage young people who are looking for guidance in their dating lives and in their marriages.

Ironically, the people with the most seasoned family resumes don't think they have anything to offer those who are just starting out. Perhaps they feel inadequate because they don't have a degree in child psychology or Christian parenting. Yet, they have so much wisdom that those just starting out long to glean from them.

Just because your own children have left the nest doesn't mean that your parenting days are over. Consider sharing the wisdom God has given you with young people in your church body. God never meant for your years of experience to go unused just because your first job is done!

ENDNOTES

INTRODUCTION

1. Alvin Toffler, *The Third Wave* (New York: Bantam Books, Inc., 1981), 211–212.

2. Toffler, *The Third Wave,* 11.

3. Toffler, *The Third Wave,* 28.

4. Toffler, *The Third Wave,* 28.

5. Toffler, *The Third Wave,* 215–216.

CHAPTER 1

Unless otherwise noted below, all material in this chapter is based on or quoted from "An Endangered Species?" a sermon by Charles R. Swindoll, July 26, 1981, or from chapter 1 of the Bible study guide The Strong Family.

1. H. Leon McBeth, *The Baptist Heritage: Four Centuries of Baptist Witness* (Nashville, Tenn.: Broadman Press, 1987), n.p.

2. Francis F. Brown, S. R. Driver, and Charles A. Briggs. *The Brown-Driver-Briggs Hebrew and English Lexicon* (Peabody, Mass.: Hendrickson Publishers, Inc., 2000), see *shanan.*

CHAPTER 2

Unless otherwise noted below, all material in this chapter is based on or quoted from "Masculine Model of Leadership," a sermon by Charles R. Swindoll, June 17, 1979, and chapter 2 of the Bible study guide The Strong Family.

1. Gerhard Kittel and Gerhard Friedrich, eds., *Theological Dictionary of the New Testament*, vol. 5, ed. and trans. Geoffrey W. Bromiley (Grand Rapids, Mich.: William B. Eerdmans Publishing Co., 1973), see *homeiromai.*

2. Timothy Friberg, Barbara Friberg, and Neva F. Miller, eds., *Analytical Lexicon of the Greek New Testament* (Grand Rapids, Mich.: Baker Books, 2000), see *homeiromai.*

3. Dan Benson, *The Total Man* (Wheaton, Ill.: Tyndale House Publishers, Inc., 1977), 178.

4. Richard C. Halverson, *Perspective: Devotional Thoughts for Men* (Grand Rapids, Mich.: Zondervan Publishing House, 1957), dedication page.

5. Benson, *The Total Man,* 183.

CHAPTER 3

Unless otherwise noted below, all material in this chapter is based on or quoted from "Positive Partner of Support," a sermon by Charles R. Swindoll, May 13, 1979, and chapter 3 of the Bible study guide The Strong Family.

1. James Dobson, *Hide or Seek: Building Self-Esteem in Your Child*, rev. ed. (Old Tappan, N.J.: Fleming H. Revell Co., 1979), 62.

2. Dobson, *Hide or Seek*, 57, 60.

3. Tim Kimmel, "Changed Lives," in *A 4th Course of Chicken Soup for the Soul: 101 More Stories to Open the Heart and Rekindle the Spirit*, ed. Jack Cranfield and others (Deerfield Beach, Fla.: Health Communications, Inc., 1997), 60–61.

4. Dobson, *Hide or Seek*, 92–93.

CHAPTER 4

Unless otherwise noted below, all material in this chapter is based on or quoted from "Your Baby Has the Bents (Part One)," a sermon by Charles R. Swindoll, April 26, 1981, or from chapter 4 of the Bible study guide The Strong Family.

1. Francis F. Brown, S. R. Driver, and Charles A. Briggs. *The Brown-Driver-Briggs Hebrew and English Lexicon* (Peabody, Mass.: Hendrickson Publishers, Inc., 2000) see *hanakh*.

2. Brown, Driver, and Briggs, *The Brown-Driver-Briggs Hebrew and English Lexicon*, see *hanakh*.

3. Note on Proverbs 22:6, *The NET Bible* (Biblical Studies Press, 2003), accessed via the Libronix Library System.

4. Laura Hillenbrand, *Seabiscuit: An American Legend* (New York: Ballantine Books, 2001), 103.

CHAPTER 5

Unless otherwise noted below, all material in this chapter is based on or quoted from "Your Baby Has the Bents (Part Two)," a sermon by Charles R. Swindoll, May 3, 1981, or from chapter 5 of the Bible study guide The Strong Family.

1. John S. Goff, *Robert Todd Lincoln: A Man in His Own Right* (Norman, Okla.: University of Oklahoma Press, 1969), 70–71.

2. Dr. A. Winship as quoted by J. Oswald Sanders, *A Spiritual Clinic* (Chicago: Moody Press, 1961), 90.

3. Max Lucado and Terri A. Gibbs, *God's Inspirational Promises* (Nashville: J. Countryman Publishers, 2001), accessed through the Libronix Library System.

CHAPTER 6

Unless otherwise noted below, all material in this chapter is based on or quoted from "A Chip Off the Old Bent," a sermon by Charles R. Swindoll, May 10, 1981, or from chapter 6 of the Bible study guide The Strong Family.

1. Beth Moore, "Is There a 'Generational Curse' for Sin?," *Today's Christian Woman* 26, no. 3 (May/June 2004), 16. Adapted by *Today's Christian Woman* from *Breaking Free* © 2000 by Beth Moore. Used by *Today's Christian Woman* with permission from Broadman & Holman. Available at http://www.christianitytoday.com/tcw/2004/003/4.16.html

CHAPTER 7

Unless otherwise noted below, all material in this chapter is based on or quoted from "Shaping the Will with Wisdom," a sermon by Charles R. Swindoll, May 24, 1981, or from chapter 7 of the Bible study guide The Strong Family.

1. Bruce A. Ray, *Withhold Not Correction* (Phillipsburg, N.J.: Presbyterian and Reformed Publishing Co., 1984), 87.

2. James Dobson, *The Strong-willed Child: Birth through Adolescence* (Wheaton, Ill.: Tyndale House Publishers, 1978), 30.

3. Dobson, *The Strong-willed Child*, 32.

4. James Dobson, *The New Hide or Seek: Building Confidence in Your Child*, rev. ed. (Grand Rapids, Mich.: Fleming H. Revell Co., 2001), 124.

CHAPTER 8

Unless otherwise noted below, all material in this chapter is based on or quoted from "Enhancing Esteem," a sermon by Charles R. Swindoll, May 17, 1981, or from chapter 8 of the Bible study guide The Strong Family.

1. Maurice Wagner, *The Sensation of Being Somebody* (Grand Rapids, Mich.: Zondervan Publishing House, 1975), 32.

2. Wagner, *The Sensation of Being Somebody*, 44–45.

3. Wagner, *The Sensation of Being Somebody*, 162.

4. Wagner, *The Sensation of Being Somebody*, 167.

5. Roy Croft, "I Love You," as quoted in *The Best Loved Poems of the American People*, selected by Hazel Felleman (Garden City, N.Y.: Garden City Publishing Co.; Garden City, N.Y.: Doubleday & Company, 1936), 25.

CHAPTER 9

Unless otherwise noted below, all material in this chapter is based on or quoted from "Challenging Years of Adolescence (Part One)," a sermon by Charles R. Swindoll, June 14, 1981, or from chapter 9 of the Bible study guide The Strong Family.

1. *Merriam-Webster's Collegiate Dictionary*, 10th ed., see "adolescence."

2. Robert L. Thomas, ed., *New American Standard Exhaustive Concordance of the Bible* (Nashville: Tenn. Holman Bible Publishers, 1981), 1518.

3. Thomas, ed., *New American Standard Exhaustive Concordance*, 1597.

4. David A. Seamands, *Putting Away Childish Things* (Wheaton, Ill.: Victor Books, 1983), 90–91.

CHAPTER 10

Unless otherwise noted below, all material in this chapter is based on or quoted from "Challenging Years of Adolescence (Part Two)," a sermon by Charles R. Swindoll, June 28, 1981, or from chapter 10 of the Bible study guide The Strong Family.

1. Jim Conway, *Men in Midlife Crisis* (Elgin, Ill.: David C. Cook Publishing, 1985), 65–68.

2. C. S. Lewis, *The Screwtape Letters* (New York: The Macmillan Company, 1958), 47.

CHAPTER 11

Unless otherwise noted below, all material in this chapter is based on or quoted from "Warning the Uninvolved," a sermon by Charles R. Swindoll, April 17, 1983, or from chapter 11 of the Bible study guide The Strong Family.

1. Eli eventually went blind by age ninety-eight (1 Samuel 4:15). Despite the decline of his physical eyesight, his spiritual eyes were as sensitive as ever. When God spoke to Samuel, Eli sensed it was the Lord and wisely instructed the young boy how to respond (1 Samuel 3:8–9).

2. Had Eli been obedient to the Law of Moses in the first place, he would have taken action that would have prevented his sons from bringing such shame upon the family, the priesthood, and the nation (see Deuteronomy 21:18–21).

3. Alexander Whyte, *Bible Characters*, vol. 1, *The Old Testament* (Grand Rapids, Mich.: Zondervan Publishing House, 1952), 218–219.

4. Dolores Curran, *Traits of a Healthy Family: Fifteen Traits Commonly Found in Healthy Families by Those Who Work with Them* (Minneapolis, Minn.: Winston Press, 1983), 7.

5. Curran, *Traits of a Healthy Family*, 13.

CHAPTER 12

Unless otherwise noted below, all material in this chapter is based on or quoted from "When Brothers and Sisters Battle," a sermon by Charles R. Swindoll, June 7, 1981, or from chapter 12 of the Bible study guide The Strong Family.

1. James Dobson, *The Strong-willed Child: Birth through Adolescence* (Wheaton, Ill.: Tyndale House Publishers, 1978), 126.

2. The number twenty includes David and Bathsheba's son who died as a result of God's judgment of their adultery (2 Samuel 12:9–19). Besides children borne by his wives, David also fathered children by his many concubines, although none are specifically named in the Scriptures (2 Samuel 5:13; 1 Chronicles 3:9).

3. Alexander Whyte, *Bible Characters*, vol. 1, *The Old Testament* (Grand Rapids, Mich.: Zondervan Publishing House, 1952), 309.

4. Dobson, *The Strong-willed Child*, 132.

CHAPTER 13

Unless otherwise noted below, all material in this chapter is based on or quoted from "Confronting the Unpleasant," a sermon by Charles R. Swindoll, May 31, 1981, and chapter 13 of the Bible study guide The Strong Family.

1. John White, *Parents in Pain: Overcoming the Hurt and Frustration of Problem Children* (Downers Grove, Ill.: InterVarsity Press, 1979), 201.

2. White, *Parents in Pain*, 204, 206.

3. Adapted from Jerry and Mary White, *When Your Kids Aren't Kids Anymore: Parenting Late-Teen and Adult Children* (Colorado Springs, Colo.: NavPress, 1989), 166–168.

4. White, *Parents in Pain*, 204–205.

5. White, *Parents in Pain*, 206.

6. White, *Parents in Pain*, 206–207.

CHAPTER 14

Unless otherwise noted below, all material in this chapter is based on or quoted from "Facing the Unforeseen," a sermon by Charles R. Swindoll, May 26, 1985, and chapter 14 of the Bible study guide The Strong Family.

1. Harold S. Kushner, *When Bad Things Happen to Good People* (New York: Avon Books, 1981), 138–139.

2. Dolores Curran, *Traits of a Healthy Family: Fifteen Traits Commonly Found in Healthy Families by Those Who Work with Them* (Minneapolis, Minn.: Winston Press, 1983), 258.

3. R. Laird Harris, Gleason L. Archer, Jr., and Bruce K. Waltke, eds., *Theological Wordbook of the Old Testament*, vol. 2 (Chicago: Moody Press, 1980), 856.

4. Curran, *Traits of a Healthy Family*, 258.

CHAPTER 15

Unless otherwise noted below, all material in this chapter is based on or quoted from "Enduring the Unbearable," a sermon by Charles R. Swindoll, June 2, 1985, and chapter 15 of the Bible study guide The Strong Family.

1. C. S. Lewis, *A Grief Observed* (New York: Bantam Books, 1961), 17, 18.

2. Alexander Whyte, *Bible Characters*, vol. 1, *The Old Testament* (Grand Rapids, Mich.: Zondervan Publishing House, 1952), 312–313.

3. Lewis, A *Grief Observed*, 73.

CHAPTER 16

Unless otherwise noted below, all material in this chapter is based on or quoted from "Anticipating the Unusual," a sermon by Charles R. Swindoll, June 9, 1985, and chapter 16 of the Bible study guide The Strong Family.

1. Adapted from David A. Seamands, *Healing for Damaged Emotions* (Wheaton, Ill.: Victor Books, 1981), 23.

2. Henry M. Morris, *The Genesis Record: A Scientific and Devotional Commentary on the Book of Beginnings* (San Diego: Creation-Life Publishers; Grand Rapids, Mich.: Baker Book House, 1982), 181.

3. Joseph Aldrich, *Lifestyle Evangelism,* 3rd ed. (Portland, Ore.: Multnomah Press, 1982), 20.

CHAPTER 17

Unless otherwise noted below, all material in this chapter is based on or quoted from "Accepting the Undeniable," a sermon by Charles R. Swindoll, July 12, 1981, and chapter 17 of the Bible study guide The Strong Family.

1. John White, *Parents in Pain: Overcoming the Hurt and Frustration of Problem Children* (Downers Grove, Ill.: InterVarsity Press, 1979), 44, 58.

CHAPTER 18

All material in this chapter is based on or quoted from "Releasing the Reins," a sermon by Charles R. Swindoll, July 5, 1981, and chapter 18 of the Bible study guide The Strong Family.

BOOKS FOR PROBING FURTHER

In the Old Testament, the word *wisdom* describes the technical skill needed in making priestly garments (Exodus 28:3), in crafting metalwork (Exodus 31:3), and in executing the strategy of battle (Isaiah 10:13). In a general sense, the word refers to the practical skill of living. And the source of this skill is the all-knowing, all-powerful God of heaven. By His wisdom God numbered the clouds (Job 38:37) and established the earth (Proverbs 3:19). He alone knows wisdom in its truest and ultimate sense (Job 28:20, 23).

Proverbs 9:10 tells us that the fear of the Lord is the beginning of wisdom, for only He can impart the wisdom that enables us to successfully weather the storms that life will inevitably bring. To help you prepare and ultimately triumph, we have compiled a list of books, all of them by able Bible teachers. May God's Word equip you and His Spirit encourage you as you continue to grow strong and wise in family life.

Dobson, James. *The New Dare to Discipline*. Carol Stream, Ill.: Tyndale House Publishers, 1996.

> Everyone with children will appreciate the balance between love and control that Dobson offers. Built on a solid biblical premise, the book is buttressed by Dobson's strong background in psychology and is replete with examples from his own case studies. This edition has been completely revised from his 1970 classic in the field of child discipline.

Dobson, James. *The New Hide or Seek: Building Confidence in Your Child*. Grand Rapids, Mich.: Revell Publishers, 2001.

> In this excellent book, Dobson exposes the false set of scales with which our society weighs individual worth. He then shows the parent and teacher how to develop a strategy for cultivating self-esteem in children. This book will do more than help you understand your child; it will help you understand the forces that shaped you into the person you are today.

Kimmel, Tim. *Grace-Based Parenting: Set Your Family Free*. Nashville, Tenn.: W Publishing Group, 2004.

> Kimmel rightly points out that parental fear often drives parents to coerce and control their children rather than mentor them into responsible adulthood. However right a parent's motives may be, rigid rules and holy checklists will only kill the concept of grace for a child. This book will help distinguish between guiding and controlling while showing parents how to love and correct their children the way God does.

Peterson, Eugene H. *Like Dew Your Youth: Growing Up with Your Teenager*. Grand Rapids, Mich.: William B. Eerdmans Publishing Co., 1994.

> Many parents dread the coming of adolescence, expecting shouting matches and rebellion. Peterson says the teen years don't necessarily have to be tumultuous but can be a wonderful time for the relationship to become deeper and more intimate than ever. This book shows parents how to create an atmosphere that encourages healthy communication, trust, transparency and, yes, even harmony.

Smalley, Gary. *The Key to Your Child's Heart: Raise Motivated, Obedient, and Loving Children*. Rev. and updated ed. Nashville, Tenn.: W Publishing Group, 2003.

> This revised and expanded edition of Smalley's classic gives parents practical advice for enjoying deep, transparent relationships with their children even after they have become angry or rebellious. Smalley offers specific guidelines for disciplining, motivating, and setting boundaries in ways that foster closeness. And he shows what makes a family close.

Barber, Cyril J. *Through the Valley of Tears: Encouragement and Guidance for the Bereaved*. Santa Ana, Calif.: Promise Publishing, Inc., 2002.

> Cyril Barber tenderly speaks to families who have suffered a tragic loss and face the task of grieving and rebuilding. Widowed husbands and wives, children who have lost a parent, and parents who have lost a child will discover practical advice to help them on the long journey to recovery.

Ordering Information

The Strong Family

If you would like to order additional Bible study guides, purchase the audio series that accompanies this guide, or request our product catalog, please contact the office that serves you.

United States and International locations:

Insight for Living
Post Office Box 269000
Plano, TX 75026-9000
1-800-772-8888, 24 hours a day, seven days a week (U.S. contacts)
International constituents may contact the U.S. office through mail queries or call 1-972-473-5136.

Canada:

Insight for Living Ministries
Post Office Box 2510
Vancouver, BC V6B 3W7
1-800-663-7639, 24 hours a day, seven days a week
info@insightcanada.org

Australia:

Insight for Living, Inc.
Suite 4, 43 Railway Road
Blackburn, VIC 3130
AUSTRALIA
Toll-free 1800 772 888 or 61 3 9877 4277, 9:00 A.M. to 5:00 P.M., Monday through Friday
info@aus.insight.org
www.insight.asn.au

Internet:

www.insight.org

Workbook Subscription Program

Bible study workbook subscriptions are available. Please call or write the office nearest you to find out how you can receive our workbooks on a regular basis.

NOTES

NOTES

NOTES